MOVIES FROM THE MANSION

A HISTORY OF PINEWOOD STUDIOS

MOVIES FROM THE MANSION

A HISTORY OF PINEWOOD STUDIOS

GEORGE PERRY

ELM TREE BOOKS
Hamish Hamilton – London

First published in Great Britain 1976
by Elm Tree Books/Hamish Hamilton Ltd
90 Great Russell Street, London WC1B 3PT

Copyright © 1976 George Perry
SBN 241 89500 6
Designed by Tewfick Codsi

Printed photolitho in Great Britain by
Ebenezer Baylis & Son Ltd
The Trinity Press, Worcester, and London

Contents

Foreword

O F THE threescore films and ten I have made, I would have taken a sizeable bet that nearly half of them were made at Pinewood. Over thirty years I find I have made only eight. Why I feel I have made many more is undoubtedly because they were all happy experiences.

It is a pleasure to go to Pinewood. Nothing has changed. They salute you at the entrance with a great big smile. The baronial hall where one has lunch has a happy staff who say 'Welcome back'. Through the dining room is the bar, where Kip Herren will do the same. Peter Rogers will arrive for his customary quarter bottle of champagne. Betty Box and Ralph Thomas with whom I once made a very happy picture will be there. And so will many others.

Hollywood is very different. You are clocked in and out by policemen. You eat in a canteen. No wine for you there. The best you can hope for is a Coke or a glass of milk. It's Pinewood for the personal touch, an added bonus in the 'best-of-run' studios.

May it never close.

Trevor Howard

Introduction

THE first time I visited Pinewood was in 1957 when I was an undergraduate at Cambridge. I had been writing a film column in *Varsity*, the weekly student newspaper, and was delighted to receive one day an invitation from The Rank Organisation to visit the Studios for a personal conducted tour.

In those carless days I recall the long grind out of London on the Piccadilly Line tube to Uxbridge, then a taxi ride into the leafy Buckinghamshire hinterland to the village of Iver, turning at the Crooked Billet roundabout into the concealed, straight road that leads up to the studios. As you approach from that direction there is a line of trees on the left, effectively masking the studios from view.

Abruptly you arrive at buildings, a large lodge house on one side of the road and a filling-station on the other, the mock-Tudor architecture bearing a family resemblance. On a grassy island a sign bearing the familiar man with a gong symbol proclaims 'Pinewood Studios'.

The day that I went there for the first time was a busy one. On one stage Hardy Kruger was escaping into a neutral America across a frozen St Lawrence, while on another I watched a thoughtful Peter Finch ready himself for a scene in *Robbery Under Arms*. Somewhere else Hugo Fregonese was directing a war story set in Marseilles called *Seven Thunders*. On the backlot were various Parisian streets built for *A Tale of Two Cities*.

Since then I have been to Pinewood many times. I have seen the costly aircraft simulators made for *The Battle of Britain*, the replica of Victorian Baker Street that was put up to feature in *The Private Life of Sherlock Holmes*. I remember Truffaut burning the books in *Fahrenheit 451* and Pola Negri resplendent in gold lamé for Disney's *The Moonspinners*. There was a skeleton of a dinosaur mounted on a truck tearing around the grounds for another Disney film, and terrifying flying monsters for *At the Earth's Core*. And how often there have been pleasant hours in good company in the panelled bar and its adjoining comfortable restaurant, the perfect place for a journalist to meet the top people of the film world. Or the deep arm-chair comfort of Theatre 7, perhaps watching the latest Bond film.

For above all, Pinewood is a place where films are made—a factory complex in rural surroundings (today no planning authority would sanction such an industrial encroachment on London's green belt) that thrives on activity. Pinewood is at its best when it's alive with action, the cameras rolling on the stages, sets being built and dismantled, plasterers and carpenters working at full tilt, the editing rooms humming, and new projects being hatched in the many production offices.

Films are a spasmodic, uncertain and knife-edge business, and stamina there today requires iron nerve, gall and a certain recklessness, but nevertheless there is no shortage of people who *want* to make films. Pinewood has been in existence for forty years, and today it stands alone as the only fully-serviced film studio in Europe, perhaps the only one in the Western world outside Hollywood, that can offer a comprehensive range of facilities to those who rent its space. The arguments as to whether or not the film industry can afford to sustain such a luxury will continue to rage, but it is clear that Pinewood has a special position and importance if films are to carry on being made in Britain. As the pound sterling shrinks in value there is renewed justification for the production of major international pictures on its stages, and Pinewood is able to cope with the biggest superbly.

The story of Pinewood is not one of untrammelled progress. On the contrary, the unhappy general history of Britain's last four decades has been intensified in the film industry, where optimism gave way to long years of wartime darkness, then the painful era of recovery with its dollar crises and austerity. The erosion of the cinema as television emerged as an even more potent mass visual medium, shattered Wardour Street more effectively than Hitler's bombs, and only in the last dozen years or so has there been a gradual *rapprochement*, with an ever-increasing number of series and specials made at Pinewood, now equipped with stages as suitable for TV as films.

There has been great investment in new stages, new equipment, new facilities, to keep Pinewood alive and viable. The men and women who work there have a determination to see that the place has a future. They want to be sure that for years to come audiences can still see that modest credit somewhere near the end of the main titles of a big film, 'Made at Pinewood Studios, London, England'.

1 Mr Boot's Dream

T HERE were once many British film studios. Some were scattered throughout the inner London districts—Hammersmith, Islington, Cricklewood, Highbury, Shepherd's Bush. Some were in the suburbs to the west—Merton, Isleworth, Teddington, Wembley, Southall, Ealing, Borehamwood. Some were located in the leafier areas that formed the so-called stockbroker belt—Beaconsfield, Walton-on-Thames, Denham, Maidenhead, Welwyn. Some were not even very near London—Brighton, Manchester, Torquay. One by one they all closed. Many were too small and badly designed to offer comprehensive facilities for the film-maker; others, such as Denham, disappeared because there was no place for them as the British film industry contracted and all but collapsed.

But then, it was never a very healthy business in which to set out to make a fortune. Historically, the troubles of the British film industry go back almost to the beginnings in the 1890s, but they consolidated during the First World War. Then the burgeoning American film industry achieved a stranglehold on the British one, which was in a woefully vulnerable state as war raged in the trenches of the Western Front. In those days films were of course silent, so that there were few problems of language in presenting a story to an audience, as only the subtitles had to be changed. But even American films would often be retitled for British consumption, the subtitle translators removing transatlantic idioms and substituting pukka British talk. The immediate post-war years were no better for the British film industry, and American products continued to dominate cinema screens.

The arrival of the talkies in the late 1920s changed all that. Alfred Hitchcock has the distinction of making the first British all-talking picture, *Blackmail*, a thriller made at British International Pictures, Elstree, much of it reshot or re-edited from a silent version that had already been virtually completed. Herbert Wilcox ran close behind, with *Wolves*, Charles

Pinewood's entrance lodge: 'half-timbered like a Home Counties road house'

Pinewood under construction—a new stage
every 21 days. (*Inset*) The administration
building takes shape

Laughton's first full-length film. Suddenly the British film industry was aware that the shared language could be used to advantage, particularly as Hollywood was undergoing traumatic upheavals as world-famous silent stars were found incapable of coherent speech.

Consequently, there was a perking-up of the ramshackle British film industry in the early 'thirties following the wild success of the inexpensive Alexander Korda film, *The Private Life of Henry VIII* in 1933. At last financiers were actually beginning to look at the cinema as a means of getting a return on investment. The exhibition side flourished, too, and every modern suburb of £375 three-bedroomed houses would find included in the development a parade of shops, with perhaps a resplendent new Odeon, built by Oscar Deutsch, or one of John Maxwell's rival ABCs. 'Going to the pictures' in that pre-television era represented an escape from the boredom of day-to-day existence for millions of people, and the cinema offered an atmosphere of luxury and high living that would normally be out of the reach of its audience. These were the years of the great depression, and films have usually done well when times were really hard. It is curious that few films then were ever made about those working classes who formed the bulk of the audience. It seemed they preferred to watch on the screen titled nit-wits cavort in white tie and tails and roar around the countryside in blown Bentleys. Such people themselves would rarely have gone to the cinema.

Into this climate came Charles Boot, a builder, chairman and managing director of Henry Boot Garden Estates, a company that had played its part in blanketing England with semi-detached desirable residences. Boot's wealth was considerable and the glamour of the film industry had beckoned since the silent days. A friend of his, Sir Auckland Geddes, had been to Hollywood in the 'twenties and returned glowing with excitement. Another colleague with good City connections, Sir John Henry, had joined Geddes and Boot in formulating a plan to build a British studio at Elstree that would rival the best in California. They had purchased land at Elstree and Boot had begun to build houses for the studio staff. It was his philosophy that the community should be self-contained, a complete company town, the workers living next door to their work. But a protracted period abroad removed Geddes from the scene. Then Boot had to make a long trip to Greece, and the project foundered. Perhaps it was just as well, for the talkie era dawned and his new studios would have been out of date as soon as they were opened. Elstree was still to become a centre of British film-making with the setting up of British International Pictures, and British and Dominions Film Corporation which had been started by a young Irish

Pinewood from the air—a factory in the leafy Buckinghamshire countryside

Left: Properties at Pinewood include flags all nations

Below: Art department model set for *Chit Chitty Bang Bang*

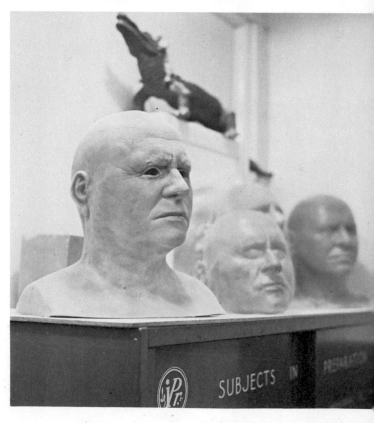

Above: Heraldic lion receives close attention

Right: Uncrowned heads have their cinematic uses

THE RESIDENCE

Heatherden Hall—the bill of sale. *Above*:
The ornamental lake and gardens, scenery
for countless films

ex-R.F.C. flier and snooker champion, Herbert Wilcox, with Nelson
Keyes.

Boot did not let his interest fade, however. He was still determined to
establish in Britain a studio that would be among the best in the world and
would attract film-makers from everywhere. His enthusiasm undiminished,
he had been to Hollywood to see for himself what the ideal requirements
for a talking-pictures studio were, and had worked out a scheme that he
felt improved on those he had seen.

Charles Boot's second opportunity came in 1934, with the death of a distinguished bankrupt named Morden. Although he had left only £10 in his
will he had once been a multi-millionaire. He had built a Buckinghamshire
mansion around an old Victorian house, sparing nothing in enlarging and
modernising it. It had earlier been the home of an Uxbridge landowner,
Dr Drury Lavin, and after that the famous Indian cricketer, K. S. Ranjit-
sinhji. Then Heatherden Hall became the home of Lt. Col. Grant Morden,
Canadian financier and Member of Parliament for Brentford and Chiswick.
Morden added a huge ballroom, a swimming pool and a Turkish bath and
laid out sixteen acres of the estate as formal gardens. It became a showplace,
the house having cost £300,000 which at that time must have seemed a
truly staggering sum. In November 1921 Heatherden Hall found a place in
history, for the treaty establishing the Irish Free State was signed there.

The mansion was situated near the village of Iver, on gravelly, wooded
heathland, about 200 feet above sea level. London was little more than 20
miles to the east, but the location was so rural and peaceful that Piccadilly
Circus might have been in another world. What made the site of Heatherden Hall particularly attractive, apart from its proximity to the capital, was
that in those days of open coal fires, it was well beyond the fog belt.

In the economic crisis of the early 'thirties Morden's fortune vanished
and at his death the estate was put up for sale. It seemed ideal for Boot's
purposes. Moreover, it was being sold off cheaply, at less than a tenth

of the £300,000 Morden had spent on it. There were nearly a hundred acres of grounds including the landscaped area around the house.

Boot first established a country club in the Hall, turning the ballroom into a restaurant and merging many of the bedrooms into furnished suites for wealthy guests. He also bought land on the opposite side of the adjoining road with the intention of building a housing estate of 400 dwellings in which the studio workers could live hard by their work. That was one of his less successful ideas; many of the houses were built, but they went on the general market at prices ranging from 14s. 5d. a week to £2. 6s. 11d. for the largest. On his return from another fact-finding mission to Hollywood Boot appointed James Sloan as general manager, and it was he who was probably the mainspring for Pinewood's then novel studio design. Sloan arranged the stages into compact units consisting of one large and one small stage adjoining with shared offices, dressing rooms and other facilities. There were to be eight such units in the original plan, each pair grouped around a covered rectangular area where the workshops, wardrobe and prop departments were to be housed, the same distance from all the stages. Unfortunately, the symmetry of the plan was just too perfect and only the first five stages were built to this pattern.

The larger ones (A, D and E) were 165ft by 110ft with 40ft by 30ft tanks, 8 feet deep, while the smaller stages (B and C) were 110ft by 82ft. All the studio buildings were linked by covered walkways, a sensible reminder that the British climate was not to be compared with that of Burbank or Culver City. There were many brilliant innovations in the original conception of Pinewood, not least that all the electrical gear was suspended from ceiling grids, ridding the floors of awkward cables. The first complete Western Electric recording system in Europe was installed.

The architect was A. F. B. Anderson and construction work began in November 1935. The building labourers toiled for 1s. 2¼d. an hour, yet achieved an astonishing rate of progress, taking 21 days to finish each stage. Boot chose the name Pinewood himself, quite deliberately letting it be an echo of its Californian rival. With commendable foresight he had the grounds wired with underground cables to enable exterior scenes to be filmed easily, taking advantage of the many scenic backgrounds that the Pinewood estate had to offer. Countless films have had scenes shot in the gardens, using the ornamental lake and bridge as a background, while the house has itself played many roles from stately home to school for spies.

The studio administration block was built behind the house, and designed to blend with the grounds. Its entrance was surrounded by a vast Elizabethan fireplace carved in solid oak and bearing the date 1581. It had been

The entrance to the administration building
—surrounded by an Elizabethan fireplace
of solid oak

bought from Allum Hall, Derbyshire when that old house was demolished
and is reputed to have taken a family of craftsmen thirty years to carve. The
Board Room was decorated with the panelling from the retired Cunard
liner, *Mauretania*, then being broken up, and was bought for a mere £78.
The entrance lodge on the Fulmer Road was built in a half-timbered style
like a Home Counties road house, and the seven projecting wings of offices
and dressing rooms on the main avenue were painted a deep oxblood to
disguise their utilitarian architecture, the prototype of many a wartime
R.A.F. station.

As Boot's ideas for Pinewood took shape a significant meeting took place. Joseph Arthur Rank was a Yorkshireman, member of the famous flour-milling family. He directed the family business in the City of London where he had acquired considerable skill in his financial dealings, and a sizeable fortune. He was also a devout Methodist. In the 'twenties he had acquired the *Methodist Times* with the intention of spreading the faith by means of the printing press. Although a city tycoon he nevertheless regularly conducted Sunday school at home in Reigate. He saw the possibilities of film as a means of disseminating religious ideas to a wider audience, and produced a twenty-minute film for the Religious Film Society, formed by him in 1933. In partnership with the wealthy big-game hunting Lady Yule, widow of a jute millionaire, and John Corfield, who had made a minor film for Butcher's, one of the lesser Wardour Street distributors, he set up British National Films in October 1934. Rank initially wanted to film *The Pilgrim's Progress*, but nothing came of the project. Instead Corfield obtained the services of Norman Walker, who had worked with British International Pictures for some five years, under the aegis of John Maxwell. A novel by Leo Walmsley about rivalry between two Yorkshire fishing families was selected, and it was filmed as *The Turn of the Tide*, with Wilfrid Lawson, Moore Marriott and the young Geraldine Fitzgerald, who was later to become a Hollywood star. The location shooting was at Robin

J. Arthur Rank and his wife in pre-war
days at their home in Reigate

Hood Bay, on the Yorkshire coast, near Whitby, and the interiors were filmed in the British and Dominions Studios at Elstree, where Herbert Wilcox was in charge.

Rank was not impressed by the studios he had seen. It seemed intolerable that work had to stop to enable sets for fresh scenes to be erected, a common problem in most cramped British film studios, some of which had only one stage. His instinct for industrial efficiency told him that what was desperately needed if Britain was to produce films with the polish and production values that would compare with the Hollywood output was a new, completely modern, planned studio complex. And that was the motivation for the meeting between Boot and Rank, the one supplying what the other needed. The first Board of Pinewood Studios consisted of Boot, Rank, Corfield—who represented Lady Yule—and Spencer Reis, who was Boot's son-in-law. Corfield was despatched to Berlin to have a look at the UFA studios and to add to the corpus of knowledge that was accumulating to influence Pinewood's design.

Early in 1936 a new injection of capital came in the shape of British and Dominions. The Elstree Studios had been partially destroyed by a disastrous fire, and having collected the insurance, the company was looking for new production facilities. They became part-owners of Pinewood, with a 50 per cent investment. The Board was thus strengthened with Ronald Crammond, the B & D chairman, Herbert Wilcox and the Hon. Richard Norton who had been in charge of production at B & D.

Norton, a descendant of the playwright Sheridan, was a stooped, monocled figure, his deformation the result of war injuries, which had not deterred him from acquiring a considerable reputation as a racing motorist. He had been through a fortune or two, and knew the avenues of European finance. His most successful stroke had been as head of production at British and Dominions, when he persuaded United Artists to back Korda's very successful *The Private Life of Henry VIII*. Norton, heir to Lord Grantley, became Pinewood's first managing director. Herbert Wilcox tells the story that he finally gained acceptance with the workers there, who had found his manner and appearance discomfiting, when on the occasion of showing C. M. Woolf around the studios he was transfixed by a very prominent graffiti message: 'The Honourable Richard Norton is a shit.' He picked up a piece of chalk and, having just been elevated with the death of his father a few days earlier, scored out 'The Honourable Richard Norton' and wrote 'Lord Grantley'.

Now Rank was to learn a hard lesson. In order to get *The Turn of the Tide* a release he had to make an unsatisfactory deal with Mark Ostrer,

Left: Anna Neagle and Robert Douglas in *London Melody*—the first sequence shot in the new studios

Randle Ayrton, Sally Eilers and Basil Sydney in Carol Reed's *Talk of the Devil*— Pinewood's first complete film

who then ran the Gaumont-British cinema circuit. It went out as the bottom half of a double bill and brought in less than half the £30,000 it had cost to make. Rank realised that it was not the producers, but the distributors and exhibitors who had the muscle when it came to determining whether or not films would be in a position to make money. To be really successful a producer would have to achieve a vertically-integrated business, that is to say, the control of production, distribution and exhibition— a formula that had been effective in the American industry although it was to be outlawed in 1947 under a Congressional Act. Rank joined C. M. Woolf, who had recently resigned from Gaumont-British after falling out with the Ostrer brothers and together they set up General Film Distributors, the first company to use the man with the gong as its symbol. The first gong-beater was Bombardier Billy Wells, a former heavyweight boxer. Later, Phil Nieman and Ken Richmond, both wrestlers, would perform for the famous trademark. GFD bought a quarter share in the American firm, Universal Pictures, which although not one of the Hollywood majors, had a few box-office assets, particularly the new young singing star, Deanna Durbin. Rank was soon able to buy out the Ostrers and gain control of the Gaumont screens. He was now poised to become the most powerful man in the history of British cinema.

Pinewood Studios rose fast. By 30 September 1936 all was ready for the opening ceremony, and 1200 guests gathered on Stage D to eat a cold lunch of Scotch salmon, Surrey chicken and York ham and to hear the speeches. Of those responsible for the new buildings the only conspicious absence was C. M. Woolf, who was too ill to attend. The ceremony was performed by the Parliamentary Secretary to the Board of Trade, Dr Leslie Burgin, who said that he had been consulting a dictionary of arboriculture, and had learned that 'compared with the majestic pine, the holly is a bush or a stunted tree'.

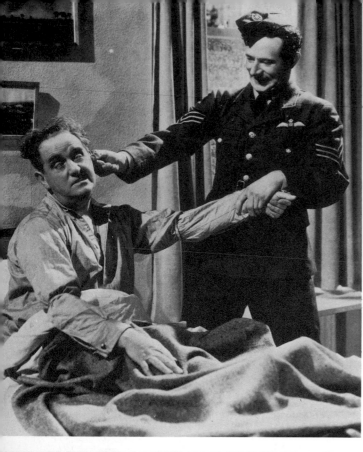

Left: Sydney Howard and Richard Hearne
in *Splinters in the Air*
Below: Richard Cromwell and Hazel Terry
have problems in *Our Fighting Navy*

Pinewood was a remarkable achievement. The first brick had been laid in the previous December; now six million bricks and nine months later the cameras were ready to turn. Miss Sally Sutherland, a publicity lady translated from B & D to Pinewood, told the awed Press: 'It's as if a millionaire with a beautiful house suddenly decided to make pictures in his garden.' Mr Boot recalled the conversation he had had on his trip to Hollywood with the fierce Louis B. Mayer, who had told him to stick to the Yorkshire pudding and roast beef—leave the sweets alone. Boot had replied, 'I like the sweets.' They had cost him a million pounds, £580,000 of which had gone to the building contractors, but on that day in September 1936 Mr Boot was happy.

'You have a wealth of imagery at your command,' said Dr Burgin. 'When you have not, you invent it.' Many of the guests, sated on Pinewood Bombe and Mumm Cordon Rouge '28, then toured the stages, pausing to watch Herbert Wilcox shoot a departure-platform scene at a mock-up of Victoria Station for *London Melody*, starring Anna Neagle and Tullio Carminatti. Historically, it was the first film to be finished at Pinewood, but as production had begun several months earlier at B & D, Elstree and come to a standstill on account of the fire, it was not the first complete Pinewood film. That distinction was to go to the young Carol Reed's *Talk of the Devil* with the imported American stars Sally Eilers and Ricardo Cortez, on opening day still known as *The Man With Your Voice*. The other inaugural productions were *Splinters in the Air*, a comedy with Sydney Howard, and *Our Fighting Navy*, directed by Norman Walker.

Kine Weekly, one of the trade papers, brought out a lavish commemorative supplement. Said its editor: 'From today Pinewood is a living entity. What can humanly be done to ensure success has been done, and there is not a man in the business but will rejoice when the point of all these labours, good British pictures, are arriving on the market.' Richard Norton also wrote in the supplement, emphasising that the essence of the Pinewood operation was 'Service'. 'For the first time in the history of British pictures,' he said, 'it will be possible in a studio for motion picture people to live with motion pictures. I can proudly claim that there is nothing in Pinewood that does not in some way or another reduce the usual waste of time and money to a bare minimum, and we are sure the word "breakdown" will be a thing of the past.'

It seemed a good time to be optimistic.

2 Pinewood Coins it

PRODUCTION at Pinewood seemed to begin well. Paramount filmed *The Scarab Murder Mystery* with Wally Patch and Wilfrid Hyde-White, and the young Margaret Lockwood starred in *Melody and Romance*, directed by Maurice Elvey, with an even younger Hughie Green as a junior radio star. In a similar vein, Herbert Wilcox brought in Ralph Reader to play in a film version of his famous annual scouting revue, *The Gang Show*. Shortly after its opening Pinewood was the busiest British studio, although at that time Amalgamated at Elstree and London Films at Denham had more stage space. British feature-film production generally reached its highest point in 1937–38 with 228 titles registered. Since the imposition of the 1927 Cinematograph Films Act the quota system had been in force, and it had transformed British production, by legislating a minimum screen time for domestically produced films. In the mid-'thirties the distributors' and exhibitors' quota was 20 per cent. Regrettably, many of the films that were then being churned out in the British studios were known as 'quota quickies' and were cheaply made, with shoddy scripts, basic direction and banal acting. Their sole purpose was to occupy screen time in order that the law be met.

Consequently, British films had a bad reputation with the film-going public, who demonstrated their disgust by ignoring the domestic product, flocking instead to the lavish Hollywood offerings of the time. It was the era of the Rogers-Astaire musicals, *Mutiny on the Bounty*, Shirley Temple, the Marx Brothers, *The Good Earth*, Jean Harlow, Clark Gable—competition on a scale that would be hard for any imitator to match. Most British films remained firmly in the bottom halves of the double bills.

Pinewood's 24 films made in 1937 included a certain number of quickies. Their short shooting schedules meant that they could be rushed through the studios in between more important productions. Nevertheless, several talented newcomers were able to cut their teeth on the more modest pictures. For instance, the screenplay of *Midnight Menace* was written by

Margaret Lockwood, a young ingénue in
Melody and Romance

Fritz Kortner has Margaret Vyner in his
clutches in *Midnight Menace*

Pinewood Coins It 31

Roger Macdougall, who was to become an eminent playwright, and Alexander Mackendrick, who would make his name as director of such Ealing films as *The Man in the White Suit* and *The Ladykillers* before going to Hollywood and *The Sweet Smell of Success*. Conversely, they were often the last efforts of veterans who had seen better things. The very last feature directed by the great pioneer of the British silent cinema, George Pearson, was a Pinewood quickie, called ominously, *The Fatal Hour*.

But Pinewood was more than a mere film factory. Its employees were entranced by the grounds and the clubhouse. The room in which the Irish Free State Treaty had been signed was turned into a cocktail bar, and the great ballroom adjoining became a spacious, panelled restaurant, with French windows alongside opening on to carefully groomed lawns. In those early days fresh vegetables grown in the kitchen gardens were served exclusively at lunch. Upstairs was an art gallery and there was a writing room, drawing room, billiards room and so on as befitted a stately home. The plumbing in particular was of an astonishing opulence. Guests could

The Heatherden Hall ballroom transformed into a luxurious restaurant—fresh-grown vegetables served daily

Bathroom in the Nell Gwyn suite: 'surroundings that would surely intimidate a discreet bather'

have a bath in the Nell Gwyn suite in a vast marble tub, flanked by ornamental lighting columns projecting bright rays into a sculpted niche, surroundings that would surely have intimidated a discreet bather.

In some ways the Pinewood sense of remoteness was actual, rather than imagined. At first there was no London Transport country bus service nearer than the Crooked Billet, a public house some fifteen minutes' walk away on the Slough–Uxbridge road, reached along the Fulmer Road (now renamed Pinewood Road), a narrow, sloping lane flanked by fields and woods. Such rural delights were not appreciated in poor weather. The journey from Uxbridge, the nearest Underground station, could take as long as the 50 minutes it had taken to get there from Piccadilly Circus on the train. There were far fewer cars among the Pinewood workers then, and access was a problem and another reason why Charles Boot had wanted his nearby housing estate to serve their needs. The bosky delights of the ornamental acreage could soon lose their attraction when the thought of the long homeward trek at the end of the day came to mind.

But these were minor problems compared with what was happening to the British film industry in 1937. Pinewood, like its nearby rival, Denham, had been opened in the previous year in a spirit of great optimism. To some extent, Alexander Korda, whose London Films controlled Denham Studios, had been responsible for the euphoria that had then prevailed. His persuasive charm had extracted vast sums of money from City institutions to finance the industry, including a million or so from Prudential Assurance to build Denham Studios. In the boom period of 1936 £4 million was lent in ten months, most of its quickly vanishing into limbo. The speculators had been wildly misled by the success of Korda's *The Private Life of Henry VIII* three years earlier, which had, after a première at New York's Radio City Music Hall, made a killing in America; they had begun to believe that British films could secure transatlantic distribution deals. By now they were beginning to see that nothing could be further from the truth—very rarely could a British film secure an American screening, and then, more often than not, only in art houses.

Talks had also been going on with the Board of Trade over the renewal of the 1927 Cinematograph Films Act, which was nearing the end of its ten-year period of implementation. It was hoped that a formula could be found to rid the industry of the quota quickies, which were polluting the quality of production, although it was realised that at least they provided work for those employed to make them. The solution was to come in the form of a minimum cost requirement for quota qualification. But early in 1937 it was clear that a crisis was imminent. Richard Norton now found it harder to attract new films to Pinewood, particularly the more important productions. Projects were announced and then postponed or cancelled. There was friction between the production side and the distributors—producers always imagine that renters take far too big a slice of the cake and in thin times these feelings come to a head.

Twickenham Studios were the first to crack. A receiver was appointed early in the year, and Julius Hagen, head of the company, announced that he was abandoning production. Then Korda seemed to be in trouble; pay cuts were put into effect at Denham. But the biggest bombshell came with the publication of the Gaumont-British figures, showing that their overdraft had gone up to £500,000. Their subsidiary, Gainsborough, at Islington, had a loss of nearly £100,000. Gaumont-British announced that they were closing down their studios at Shepherd's Bush, folding up Gaumont-British Distributors, switching feature distribution of Gainsborough Films and that of the Gaumont-British newsreel to Rank's General Film Distributors. This move made GFD the largest British renter and on a par with the American firms operating in Wardour Street. C. M. Woolf now made his peace with the Ostrer brothers, but his price was a steep one. He agreed that GFD, in return for taking half the risk, would allow Maurice Ostrer to make a few films at the Gainsborough Studios, Islington, but that all other production was to be transferred to Pinewood. This included *Young and Innocent*, a Hitchcock thriller in the great series he made for Gaumont-British in the 'thirties, and *Gangway* and *Sailing Along*, musicals with Jessie Matthews.

Woolf also wanted to rationalise the link between GFD and British National, a move which appealed to J. Arthur Rank as it meant a tidying up of his interests in both companies. Lady Yule, however, was greatly displeased. There was a parting of the ways—Rank left British National and Lady Yule, with John Corfield, left Pinewood. In possession of her shares, Rank became chairman of Pinewood Studios Ltd, with Ronald Crammond as vice-chairman, Richard Norton as managing director, and C. M. Woolf now on the Board. Norton in particular was not unhappy at the departure of the eccentric Lady Yule, who had been worrying him unduly over some deer she had placed in the Pinewood grounds and which she constantly alleged were not being properly fed. C. M. Woolf was to be Rank's most powerful and influential colleague during his early years in the film industry, and but for his death in 1941, the subsequent history of The Rank Organisation might have been very different. The two men were a strange contrast—the one a typical, hustling Wardour Street figure, admittedly with rather more talent and acumen than most, the other a grave, pious Methodist, imbued with idealistic motives and often apparently remote from the conflicts of business dealing.

Sadly, Woolf could not get on with Norton. He felt that the stooped, monocled Etonian had no place in the film business, and he made little secret of his views. But Norton was tougher than he appeared. He was now fully stretched trying to keep the giant studios, still only a few months old, occupied, and he set up Pinebrook Ltd as an attempt to make films on a co-operative basis. There were even times when only Norton's personal cajoling induced the bank to meet Pinewood's weekly wage bill. Herbert Wilcox, who had moved to Pinewood from Elstree in spite of apprehensions concerning the overheads resulting from carpeted offices and good plumbing in the dressing rooms, was himself having financial difficulties. His films, like so many others, were just not making money. He would later in the year find the solution to his troubles, in the form of *Victoria the Great*, but alas, it was not a film made at Pinewood.

Among those that were made there in 1937 were Wilcox's *Sunset in Vienna*, directed by Norman Walker with Tullio Carminatti and Lilli Palmer, and *The Frog*, directed by Jack Raymond from the Edgar Wallace original, with Gordon Harker and a young Jack Hawkins in the cast. Jack Buchanan who, like so many performers in British films of the 'thirties, was an even more prominent stage star, played the lead in *Smash and Grab* with Elsie Randolph and in *The Sky's the Limit*, both of which he produced himself. For the latter he brought the continental singing star Mara Loseff to England. He also produced but did not appear in *Sweet Devil*, a starring vehicle for Bobby Howes, with Jean Gillie as his leading lady. Buchanan's fourth Pinewood production was *Break The News*, the second British film to be directed by René Clair (in 1935 he had made *The Ghost Goes West* for Korda), and for this Ruritanian musical Buchanan also brought Maurice Chevalier over from France. Musicals were standard fare

Spectacle for *Chitty Chitty Bang Bang*, with a lighter-than-air dirigible

in Pinewood's pre-war days, again drawing on the West End theatre in the main. Arthur Tracy (the Street Singer) made *Command Performance* and *Follow Your Star*, Walter Forde directed a galaxy of cabaret stars including Florence Desmond and Ambrose and his orchestra in *Kicking the Moon Around*. But by far the most important were *Gangway* and *Sailing Along*, starring the vivacious, high-kicking Jessie Matthews, the most successful singing actress of those years, and directed by her husband, Sonnie Hale. *Sailing Along* was the best of the three musicals he made with her, and was about a bargee's daughter with aspirations to go on the stage. Her dancing partner was Jack Whiting, and the backup included the splendid talents of Roland Young, Athene Seyler and Alastair Sim.

Then there was *Young and Innocent*. In his half-century of film directing and 53 films Alfred Hitchcock has made two at Pinewood. The second was *Frenzy* in 1971. *Young and Innocent*, adapted by Charles Bennett from Josephine Tey's *A Shilling for Candles*, is Hitchcock's favourite among his British films—a classic pursuit plot in which a young man wrongly accused of murder (Derrick de Marney) befriends a girl (Nova Pilbeam). Together they track down the real killer as they elude the police. Hitchcock utilised Pinewood's special facilities in one bravura effect. The couple find their suspect playing the drums in a blackface band at a South Coast *thé dansant*. On one of the large Pinewood stages the camera tracked in on a crane across the crowded dance floor. From a distance of 145 feet it came to a stop a mere four inches from the twitching eye of the drummer. 'It took us two days to do that one shot,' Hitchcock told François Truffaut for his famous book on the master of suspense.

In 1938 the first Pinebrook films were released; they included *A Spot of Bother*, a Vernon Sylvaine farce with Robertson Hare and Alfred Drayton, directed by David Macdonald, the same director's tautly-paced *This Man is News* with Barry K. Barnes and Valerie Hobson, and *Lightning Conductor*, directed by Maurice Elvey. Carol Reed directed Jessie Matthews in a non-singing role opposite Michael Redgrave in *Climbing High*, and Redgrave starred with Elisabeth Bergner in *Stolen Life*, directed by her husband, Dr Paul Czinner. Monty Banks also directed his famous wife Gracie Fields in *Keep Smiling*. Thornton Freeland's version of the farcical *So This is London* starred Drayton and Hare with, further down the cast list, George Sanders and a very young Stewart Granger. Lupino Lane filmed *Lambeth Walk*, the cinema version of his Victoria Palace musical *Me and My Girl*. At Pinewood it was Sally Gray. And Gordon Harker repeated a role he had made famous on the radio, *Inspector Hornleigh*. A relative failure was an attempt to film Gilbert and Sullivan, *The Mikado*

Pinewood's tank in use for *The Heroes of Telemark*, directed by Anthony Mann

Right: Jessie Matthews, Britain's leading
musical star in *Gangway*, with Barry McKay
and (*left*) in *Sailing Along*
Below: Arthur Tracy (The Street Singer)
in *Follow Your Star*

Couples: Wendy Hiller and George
Galleon in *Lancashire Luck* (*top*); Elsie
Randolph and Jack Buchanan in a censorship
bedroom in *Smash and Grab* (*centre*); Jean
Gillie and Bobby Howes in *Sweet Devil*

with Kenny Baker. It was the first film to be made at Pinewood in Technicolor. The process required a special camera then, which exposed three separate strips of film simultaneously. It was a bulky object, but engineered to Rolls-Royce standards of perfection. Early Technicolor required much more intensive lighting with a corresponding effect on the budget. *The Mikado* also featured more than 750 different costumes.

It was now time for another Hungarian to come on to the scene. Like Korda, Gabriel Pascal had been involved in quota quickies before reaching the respectable cinema. Like Korda he was dynamic, persuasive and charming. With rare *chutzpah* he bearded the great George Bernard Shaw one day at his apartment in Whitehall Court, and came away with the film producer's holy grail, screen rights on one of his most celebrated plays. Since an unfortunate experience early in the 'thirties G.B.S. had held the cinema in contempt. Then a badly-directed version of *How He Lied to Her Husband* had been released, which, because it was bereft of any Shavian wit or buoyancy, had died at the box office, taking with it even the modest investment of its author. Now Pascal achieved what had been denied to many others who had made overtures, Korda included. It seemed that Pascal knew exactly the degree of flattery and shrewdness with which to win him over. As Shaw later said: 'Pascal is doing for the films what Diaghilev did for the Russian ballet. Until he descended on me out of the clouds, I could find nobody who wanted to do anything with my plays on the screen but mutilate them, murder them, give their cadavers to the nearest scrivener . . . When Gabriel appeared out of the blue, I just looked at him, and handed him *Pygmalion* to experiment with.'

Having permission to film *Pygmalion* was one thing, but finding the money with which to do it was another. Pascal next approached Nicholas Davenport, a cultured financier, who got together a syndicate and raised the first £10,000. They then went to C. M. Woolf at GFD for a distribution contract to provide the rest of the £50,000 they estimated for the budget. Woolf turned it down. As far as he was concerned Pascal was an unknown and he was not all that impressed with the Shavian film track record. It was a typical Wardour Street brush-off and one likely to be repeated at other companies. But Pascal, through Woolf's cunning rival, Richard Norton, secured an interview with Rank, who was unaware of the

Left: Hitchcock's famous crane shot in
Young and Innocent, tracking 145 feet to a
four-inch close-up.
Above: Nova Pilbeam and Derrick de
Marney in a scene from the film,
Hitchcock's favourite pre-war
British picture
Below: Jack Hawkins and Gordon Harker
arrest Cyril Smith in *The Frog*, directed by
Jack Raymond

Above: Aldwych farceurs Alfred Drayton and Robertson Hare in *A Spot of Bother*
Below: Jack Buchanan teamed with Maurice Chevalier in *Break the News*, directed by René Clair
Opposite: Poster for *This Man is News*

INEBROOK LIMITED PRESENTS
THIS MAN IS NEWS
Civic Leaders Plan Campaign Against Gangs
Crime King
Starring
BARRY K. BARNES
and
VALERIE HOBSON
ALASTAIR SIM
with
Directed by David MacDonald · · A Paramount Release

Gordon Harker as the *Lightning Conductor*,
with Sally Gray

previous decision. Rank gave his approval, subject to guarantors being
found if the film went over budget. Woolf backed down, and a new company with Norton and Davenport on the board was formed. The most
prestigious of Pinewood's pre-war productions was then scheduled.

Pascal selected Leslie Howard to play Higgins and to direct the film. He
was another Hungarian as it happened, although few people ever realised
it, so convincing and quintessentially English was his appearance and
understated manner. However he was not happy at the thought of directing
himself, and asked for Anthony Asquith, then neglected to the extent that
he was almost on the point of abandoning films altogether and joining the
new medium of television recently started by the BBC. Wendy Hiller was
cast to play Eliza and Wilfrid Lawson, Doolittle. Pascal's pledge not to
change any dialogue without Shaw's permission soon came under challenge when Leslie Howard declared that the play would have to be opened
up for the screen. He felt particularly that the début of Eliza at the recep-
tion should be shown, not merely reported. Asquith found himself having
lunch at Whitehall Court, stricken with nerves at the terrifying prospect of
having to read a draft of the new scene to the great man, who seemed to

talk about everything else but *Pygmalion*. Finally the moment came, and the addition was accepted without demur.

Shooting proceeded reasonably smoothly, although there were moments when Pascal demonstrated the fussiness for detail that was eventually to give him the reputation for being the most extravagant of all British film-makers. On one occasion, when shooting was taking place on a Sunday in order to catch up on an over-running schedule, he objected to the plumpness of a parrot Doolittle was carrying in longshot. Doolittle's parrot, he averred, would have been skinnier. Asquith argued that it hardly showed, that thin parrots were hard to come by on a Sunday and, playing his trump card, that Pascal himself had approved this particular bird the day before. 'I did not agree,' came the Hungarian's retort. 'I protested, but you rolled on me.' Henceforth 'rolled on' became the standard Pinewood way for saying 'overruled'.

Pygmalion went over its budget only by the amount Rank had wisely asked to be guaranteed before production began. It was, however, a triumph at the box office, and caused queues to form on Broadway, a sight unprecedented for a British film since *The Private Life of Henry VIII*. Howard's cold, aloof Higgins established itself as the archetype until the play was set to music by Lerner and Loewe in the mid-'fifties. In Britain there was still considerable shock value in the heroine letting forth a 'Not bloody likely' in the context of polite conversation, and the film was talked about incessantly, especially by radio comedians looking for quick laughs. The exultant Pascal, now a hero, announced that he would direct his next Shaw film, *Major Barbara*, which was to be made at Denham.

The situation at Denham Studios had become very unhappy. Courageously, Korda had been pouring money into spectacular films such as *The Drum* and *The Four Feathers*, made in Technicolor, greatly adding to production costs. But the time had come when with no more money forthcoming and London Films' liabilities now around £1 million he could keep his studios no longer. The Prudential seized them and after negotiations a deal was set up between them, Woolf, Norton and Rank, whereby Korda could continue production but only as a tenant in his former studios, which were now controlled by his arch-rivals. A new company was formed, Denham and Pinewood Studios Ltd, with Crammond, Norton, Rank, Boot, Spencer Reis, Sir Connop Guthrie and Edward H. George of London Films, and E. H. Lever, the Secretary of the Prudential. Norton had, it is assumed, been the one responsible for the merger, working on the old financial principle of debt consolidating. The man who owes a lot is more

ELISABETH BERGNER · MICHAEL REDGRAVE

STOLEN LIFE

Produced and Directed by PAUL CZINNER . . . A Paramount Release

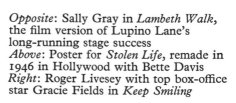

Opposite: Sally Gray in *Lambeth Walk*, the film version of Lupino Lane's long-running stage success
Above: Poster for *Stolen Life*, remade in 1946 in Hollywood with Bette Davis
Right: Roger Livesey with top box-office star Gracie Fields in *Keep Smiling*

Above: Berton Churchill, Alfred Drayton,
Robertson Hare and George Sanders in
So This Is London
Below: Gordon Harker and Alastair Sim in
Inspector Hornleigh

Pinewood's first Technicolor film, *The Mikado*,
with Sidney Granville and Martin Green

important to his creditors than the man who owes a little. Pinewood's
liabilities were now added to those of Denham.

It was however the end of pre-war film-making at Pinewood. Henceforth
production was to be confined to Denham. A further addition to the Rank
studio empire was made in 1939 when the Amalgamated Studios at Elstree
came under the control of his General Cinema Finance Corporation. There
was now far more studio space at his disposal than films to be made, but the
worsening international situation was dwarfing such problems, and the new
acquisition was soon leased to the Ministry of Works for storage, at 4 per
cent return on capital. Rank had also enlarged his exhibition interests and
joined the board of Odeon Theatres, after injecting fresh capital to enable
Oscar Deutsch to take over the Paramount circuit, a small but important
group of key site houses. In a few adroit moves Rank had become the
colossus of the British film industry, although four years earlier he had
scarcely started to get involved.

Two men now joined him who would be important figures in the Rank
story. Earl Sheffield St John was a First World War doughboy who had not
returned to America but stayed to become the Paramount circuit's general

Leslie Howard with Wendy Hiller in
Gabriel Pascal's production of Shaw's
Pygmalion. Howard remained the definitive
Professor Higgins until *My Fair Lady*

manager. The other was John Davis, a young accountant brought in to
sort out the muddled Odeon books.

War came on 3 September 1939. The government, fearing massive
enemy air assaults, immediately closed all places of entertainment. When
the raids did not materialise they were re-opened. But the number of
British film studios in production shrank from 22 before the war to a mere
9. Amalgamated was already in official hands, and now Pinewood was
requisitioned. The great stages became warehouses for flour and sugar,
emergency food supplies to feed a starving, bomb-crazed nation; happily
the eventuality did not arise. More intriguing was the establishment of an
out-station, in 'hush-hush' conditions, of the Royal Mint. As the copper
coins came pouring out, so the joke went around that Pinewood was for the
first time making money. Lloyds also moved wartime staff there when their
City offices were bombed.

But for Gabriel Pascal, Denham might have closed too. During the
worrying period in 1940 when space was desperately needed to build
fighters in vast numbers to quell the all-conquering Luftwaffe, a team from
Lord Beaverbrook's Ministry of Aircraft Production scoured Britain looking for suitable large buildings to turn into aircraft factories. At Denham
they found Pascal only halfway through *Major Barbara*, the ten-week
schedule having doubled in length. They went away, and by the time the
film was finished the 1940 emergency was over. Denham was thus able to
remain open throughout the war, providing many major films including
Noël Coward's *In Which We Serve* and Pascal's *Caesar and Cleopatra*.

Apart from a few training films made by the Crown Film Unit and the
War Office in the latter part of the war Pinewood was out of the industry.

3 Post-War Optimism

OFFICIALLY, Pinewood was not re-opened as a film studio until 4 April 1946, eleven months after the war in Europe came to an end. The task of derequisitioning the buildings had proceeded smoothly enough, although the deep red paint of the administration building and the dressing rooms and offices facing it had been replaced by the wild abstract swirls of wartime camouflage.

The war years had seen the Rank interests multiply even further. Oscar Deutsch of Odeon had died in 1941 and C. M. Woolf in 1942. The Odeon circuit was now fully controlled by Rank as indeed was the Gaumont-British circuit, although they were still run separately. Together they made a total of 619 Rank cinemas, with ABC, the rivals, owning a further 442. Between them the two groups controlled more than a third of the total seating throughout the country, and had the additional advantage of having most of their theatres in better positions and in better condition than those of the independents. The government, worried by the size of this duopoly, had set up the Palache Committee in 1944, which had recommended legislation to prevent a merger between Rank and ABC. Their Report was anxious that the British film industry, however, should be protected from an American takeover, and asked for direct government participation in films, in effect for a body like the National Film Finance Corporation to be set up. 'A cinematograph film,' said the Report, 'represents something more than a mere commodity to be bartered against others. Already the screen has great influence, both politically and culturally, over the minds of the people. Its potentialities are vast, as a vehicle for expression of national life, ideals and tradition, as a dramatic and artistic medium, and as an instrument for propaganda.'

In 1944 Rank had bought out the Prudential interest in D & P Studios, and now with Amalgamated at Elstree he received income from the three

Alastair Sim and Trevor Howard in *Green for Danger*: murder in a wartime hospital. The first film completed in the re-opened Pinewood

largest studios in the country without the necessity of having to make films in two of them. Rank also controlled the Gainsborough Studios at Islington, the re-opened Lime Grove Studios at Shepherd's Bush, and had an arrangement to distribute the films made by Ealing. The various fiscal arrangements by which the Rank empire had been put together were more like crazy paving than straightforward building blocks, and companies proliferated and branched out to such a degree that few, other than financial experts, could see how it was done. It was the work of someone with an inborn genius for tycoonery.

But J. Arthur Rank was essentially a humane tycoon. He believed passionately in British films and wanted to see them shown in all the major film markets of the world. Throughout the war his interests had been coalescing with the aim of establishing in the post-war world a British film industry that could and would rival Hollywood. He had financed a number of films that had made an impression abroad, even in America, although in cost terms they had been major productions. Olivier's *Henry V*, for instance, completed in 1944, absorbed £475,000 of Rank's money; but it was to earn it all back and more, as well as bringing international distinction to Britain. Even more expenditure at the height of the war was lavished on Gabriel Pascal's version of Shaw's *Caesar and Cleopatra*, a Denham film that eventually was to cost £1,278,000, a sum that included location shooting in Egypt and a massive reconstruction in England of ancient Alexandria. It was the most expensive British film ever made, a distinction retained for many years afterwards. Pascal ended the film in hospital, having been nibbled by a camel, and Rank, now aware that he was being taken for a ride, cancelled the profligate producer's next film, which was to have been *Saint Joan*.

Another emigré who had a powerful influence on Rank in his war and immediate post-war period was Filippo del Giudice, who had arrived in England some years before as a refugee from Mussolini's Italy who was already in his forties but without a word of English. He lived off the proceeds of Italian lessons given to the children of Soho waiters and by 1937 had become sufficiently established to set up a modest film company, Two Cities (they were London and Rome). When the war started he was interned, but he was released in September 1940. A few months later he perpetrated a coup of the magnitude of Pascal's cornering of Shaw. He went to Noël Coward and persuaded him to make a film about the navy. Coward had demurred at first, but after hearing of the exploits of his friend, Lord Mountbatten, whose destroyer, H.M.S. *Kelly*, had been sunk off Crete, he decided to accept del Giudice's proposal on condition that he be given total artistic control, including writing the script and playing the lead. Del

Oscar Deutsch's Odeons—allegedly 'Oscar Deutsch Entertains Our Nation'.
Left: Brighton
Below: The flagship—Leicester Square, in 1945

Giudice was delighted, but actually did not have enough money to go ahead. C. M. Woolf agreed to offer a distribution contract, but later backed out, although shooting had already begun on borrowed money at Rank's Denham Studios. British Lion eventually took the film over and released it. In spite of its costs, *In Which We Serve* was one of the most successful British war films, taking two million dollars in America and giving a cinematic start to many major names such as Richard Attenborough, who played a panic-stricken stoker, David Lean, who began his directorial career co-directing with Coward, Ronald Neame, who was the cameraman, and David Rawnsley the art director, who was to mastermind Pinewood's controversial Independent Frame system a few years later.

Del Giudice had a simple formula for success. 'Spend money! British films in the past have been poor only because they were cheap.' After *In Which We Serve* del Giudice was a respected figure in Wardour Street. Subsequent Two Cities films were made at Denham—the Coward stories *This Happy Breed* and *Blithe Spirit* and *Henry V*, which Rank financed in exchange for control of the company. Del Giudice now had an important position of power and influence, and with C. M. Woolf no longer alive to curb his extravagance he was able to initiate many expensive productions, some of which had no hope of financial success.

But in 1946 there were few Jeremiahs. David Lean's *Brief Encounter* had been followed by a brilliant version of a Dickens novel, *Great Expectations*,

Green for Danger, with Ronald Adam,
Alastair Sim, Sally Gray, Leo Genn
and Trevor Howard

Great Expectations, with John Mills, directed by David Lean, who cleverly exploited bomb-damaged London. *Above*: Finlay Currie as Magwitch, confronts Anthony Wager as the young Pip

which had brought Alec Guinness to the screen in a minor role. Lean was a member of Independent Producers Ltd, a company that had been established at Pinewood under the Rank umbrella in order to take external pressure off the shoulders of creative film-makers so that they would have more energy for artistic expression. Such idealism seems almost naïve today, and even in those days it was remarkable. Alan Wood in his excellent biography *Mr Rank* quotes Lean as saying: 'I doubt if any other group of film-makers anywhere in the world can claim as much freedom. We of Independent Producers can make any subject we wish, with as much money as we think that subject should have spent upon it. We can cast whatever actors we choose, and we have no interference at all in the way the film is made. No one sees the films until they are finished, and no cuts are made without the consent of the director or producer, and what's more, not one of us is bound by any form of contract. We are there because we want to be there. Such is the enviable position of British film-makers today, and such are the conditions which have at last given our films a style and nationality of their own.' It seemed too good to be true, and amazing that Rank was not given the runaround to a far greater extent than he was by some of the more unscrupulous persons gathered around him. Independent Producers, were, however, men of integrity. The original members (the company was set up in the middle of the war) were Marcel Hellman, Leslie Howard (who died mysteriously in a plane crash soon after), David Lean, Anthony Havelock-Allen and Ronald Neame (who had their own production group, Cineguild), Ian Dalrymple (Wessex), Frank Launder and Sidney Gilliat (Individual Pictures), Michael Powell and Emeric Pressburger (The Archers). James Sloan was the general manager, and Tom White chief production manager. In 1945 George Archibald became managing director.

At Gainsborough, the production company that Rank had acquired with Gaumont-British, the output under Ted Black had concentrated on a very commercial section of the market, particularly in the field of gothic melodramas of *The Man in Grey, Madonna of the Seven Moons, The Wicked Lady* calibre. Margaret Lockwood and James Mason had become the top box-office British stars on the strength of their Gainsborough work, and constituted another jewel in the Rank crown. Black left Gainsborough at the time of *The Wicked Lady* after quarrels with Maurice Ostrer, who in turn left in the following year, having failed to agree with Filippo del Giudice's ill-conceived plans to integrate all the productions in the Rank empire. Sydney Box was then put in charge at Gainsborough, after making a hit with a Rank-distributed film *The Seventh Veil*, which had been shot at the small Riverside Studios at Hammersmith.

Above: Stewart Granger, a major box-office
star in 1947, takes up arms in *Captain
Boycott*
Right: *Captain Boycott*, Launder and
Gilliatt's study of the Irish evictions,
filmed on location in County Mayo

A company that del Giudice was unable to get his hands on was Ealing,
which was run very effectively by Michael Balcon, who apart from being
one of Rank's most powerful critics (to some extent the Palache Committee
of 1944 was established in order to examine some of his revelations of
monopolistic practices) was a major figure in the industry. He had secured
from Rank an excellent deal whereby Ealing would have total autonomy of
production and independence, circuit release, good distribution terms and
representation on the Rank Board, while Rank had a 50 per cent stake
(later increased to 75 per cent) in Ealing Films. Balcon, in his autobiography, acknowledges that it was a model contract 'leaning, if anything, to
the generous side on the part of the Rank Organisation.'

Launder and Gilliat were the first to complete a film in the re-opened
Pinewood Studios. *Green for Danger* was in essence a murder mystery set in
a hospital, with doodlebugs punctuating the action. Rosamund John, Sally
Gray and Judy Campbell were nurses, Trevor Howard a doctor, Leo Genn
a suave surgeon and Alastair Sim a wily detective who cracked the case.
While modest, it was a fair enough start to the new Pinewood era. The
same team later made *Captain Boycott*, an examination of the Irish tenancy
disputes of the 1880s with Cecil Parker as the eponymous landlord whose
name passed into the language. While it ought to have fitted into the
climate of the new socialist Britain, it somehow did not appeal to the general
taste and was a box-office failure. The other two productions inaugurating

Right: Identity parade in *Take My Life*
Below: Greta Gynt arrives at a studio-built
country hotel

post-war Pinewood were *Take My Life*, a Cineguild thriller directed by David Lean, an unusual subject for him as he had by now become associated with screen versions of Coward and Dickens, and The Archers' (Michael Powell and Emeric Pressburger) Technicolor film, *Black Narcissus*, photographed with distinction by Jack Cardiff. It was the second Technicolor film to be made at Pinewood, and as there were only four of the massive cameras needed to shoot with the old three-strip method available in Britain, not many were capable of being made. Powell and Pressburger's previous film, *A Matter of Life and Death*, for which a gigantic escalator had been specially built at Denham, was also in colour and was chosen to have its première in November 1946 at the first of what were to be annual Royal Film Performances. *Black Narcissus* won Academy Awards in 1948 for art direction and photography. The story was taken from a Rumer Godden novel about a group of Anglo-Catholic nuns battling in the Himalayas against native superstition as they attempt to run a school and hospital. Deborah Kerr and David Farrar were the chief stars and Jean Simmons played a hoydenish young Indian girl clad in brightly-coloured wrap-round skirts, which contrasted with the flowing white habits of the nuns. A former child star and product of the Aida Foster stage school, Jean Simmons was still only 17 at the time but was regarded as one of the most important potential British stars, a promise that happily she was later to fulfil.

The Archers' next film, a black-and-white work called *The End of the River* and set in South America, was made largely on location, directed by Derek Twist, and was a disappointment. But the following film represented a considerable landmark in British film-making. *The Red Shoes* gave Rank initial worries—the proposed budget was £380,000. On the promise that it be reduced to an acceptable £325,000 production began, but it was soon clear that the sum was inadequate. There followed the inevitable dilemma —was it better to call a halt and cut losses, or let them ride? Luckily, the latter course of action prevailed, and although the film was eventually to cost more than £500,000 it became the highest-earning British film to be screened in America, an accolade it held for many years.

A ballet story, it brought the beautiful red-headed ballerina Moira Shearer to the screen. While the story of a dancer torn between a ruthless Diaghilev-type impresario (Anton Walbrook) and a tormented young composer (Marius Goring) was somewhat trite and melodramatic, the back-

Left: *Black Narcissus*: Deborah Kerr, at left, and on the right, Flora Robson

Below: *The Red Shoes*: Marius Goring as the young composer with Moira Shearer, an ill-fated ballerina
Right: Moira Shearer dances with a newspaper—an effect achieved by the 'Gunshot' technique

Preceding pages: Alec Guinness as Fagin,
John Howard Davies as Oliver, in David
Lean's *Oliver Twist*
Top: Robert Newton as Bill Sikes in a
scene with Alec Guinness
Right: The closing scene of *Oliver Twist*
goes before the cameras—the Pinewood
backlot

ground of the life of a great company with the devoted attention to constant
practice and rehearsal gave an impression of realistic observation. Addi-
tionally, there was a complete ballet in the film, composed by Brian Easdale
and choreographed by Robert Helpmann, which allegorised the film's plot.
The colour photography by Jack Cardiff and the art direction by Hein
Heckroth added to the film's distinction. The Pinewood technicians found
themselves doing many fresh things—fading lights from music cues, aiming
a 300amp spotlight beam at the dancers. It was the first British film to be
lit by 'Brutes', gigantic arcs that could light an entire *corps-de-ballet* from
one source, and another innovation was the 'Gunshot' travelling-matte,
used in the ballet sequence to simulate Moira Shearer dancing with a
newspaper, for instance, and so named after its inventor George Gunn,
who was the head of Technicolor's camera department in Britain.

There were two classic British films made at Pinewood in 1947, *The Red
Shoes*, and *Oliver Twist*. The latter was made by David Lean and Cineguild,
as a follow-up to his 1946 success, *Great Expectations*. Alec Guinness had
made a powerful début in the earlier film in the relatively small role of
Herbert Pocket, and now Lean exploited his acting gifts to the full, allowing
him to create a Fagin so vividly effective that the film was promptly banned
in the United States on the grounds of anti-Semitism. It had been antici-
pated that there might be trouble on that score, but nevertheless Lean was
allowed to get on with it his way, even though it meant a substantial loss of
revenue. Lean, and his cinematographer Ronald Neame, staged an immensely effective opening sequence showing Oliver's mother just before

Back projection in action—Pinewood has
perfected the ancient film technique

Complicated set-up for *Live and Let Die*, as the Panavision camera shoots the reflection over James Bond's bed

notable performances in the film were given by Robert Newton as an eyeball-rolling Bill Sikes, Francis L. Sullivan as Mr Bumble the Beadle, and Kay Walsh as Nancy. A young Anthony Newley played the Artful Dodger and also in the cast was a 16-year-old Diana Dors who, having changed her name from Diana Fluck, had made her film debut a year earlier in *The Shop at Sly Corner*. Oliver was played by John Howard Davies, now an eminent BBC television director.

Regrettably, Cineguild's impeccable record was to be marred by their other 1947 picture, *Blanche Fury*, a costumed melodrama directed by Marc Allegret, which although stylishly photographed by Guy Green, amounted to little. However, it must be said, Valerie Hobson and Stewart Granger scowled nicely.

Ian Dalrymple's Wessex Films were responsible for the remaining two 1947 films shot at Pinewood. The first, *The Woman in the Hall*, starred Ursula Jeans as a woman who acquired money and marriage through confidence trickery, and Jean Simmons as her daughter, drawn into the deceit. The other was *Esther Waters*, a turgid adaptation of George Moore's Victorian novel with a background of life below stairs and horse racing. Neither film was very successful, the first in spite of Jack Lee's direction and the second hardly saved by a reasonably careful reconstruction of the Derby won by Fred Archer, the most celebrated Victorian jockey. *Esther Waters* was, however, notable in one respect. It brought to the screen in the leading male role a young actor who was to be a major Rank contract star. Dirk Bogarde was the son of *The Times* art correspondent, a Hampstead Dutchman, and became an actor after a spell as a commercial artist. He had been signed by Rank after excellent notices in a West End play with Kenneth More, *Power Without Glory*, and was originally scheduled to play a lesser role in Ian Dalrymple's film, with Stewart Granger in the lead. Granger dropped out belatedly and Bogarde was hastily substituted.

Rank's campaign for a major British film industry was conducted on many fronts. A British answer to the American series *The March of Time*, a regular news feature magazine, was started up under the title *This Modern Age*, each monthly issue being two reels or twenty minutes in length. It attracted considerable prestige and awards for its journalism, but was never able to pay for itself. Rank also started an animated films division at Cookham, under the control of David Hand, who had been one of Disney's key men. There was no need for Disney to have worried; the project was unsuccessful and was to cost Rank half a million pounds. At Shepperton another million had been squandered on a British attempt at a Hollywood supermusical, called *London Town*, directed by Wesley Ruggles,

Dirk Bogarde with Lalage Lewis in *Esther Waters*, his first film

A scene from *The Woman in the Hall*

specially imported from Hollywood. Shot in inadequate studios which had only just been derequisitioned, the film was a dismal failure. In any case, Ruggles had a reputation for comedies, and had never made a musical before. Rank wanted to fill his cinemas with all-Rank programmes, including the B pictures, or second features. He bought the small Highbury Studios and installed John Croydon as producer. It was hoped that Highbury would form a training ground for new talent, and to this end a 'Charm School' was established there, a group of young starlets who on salaries of £20 a week were groomed for stardom. Unfortunately, the choice of girls was uninspired and the public remained uninterested.

Rank also acquired theatres abroad. He bought the Winter Garden in New York to be his Broadway showcase. He started a circuit in Canada and purchased others in Australia and New Zealand. But he still lacked booking power in America, and distribution costs were so high that the returns on even a successfully received film such as *Great Expectations* were too low to be healthy.

And then there was the Independent Frame experiment, of which more will be told. It was hardly surprising that in spite of the immediate post-war euphoria, losses on film production alone in 1946 came to £1,667,000 and that by the autumn of 1947 when the figures were known, shudders were rippling through The Rank Organisation. Yet even worse was to come.

John Laurie and Gordon Jackson in
Floodtide, an Independent Frame film

4 Hard Times

BRITAIN in 1947 was undergoing a severe balance of payments crisis. Something in the order of £18 million was leaving the country destined for the pockets of American film producers showing their films in British cinemas, at a rate of more than a million dollars a week. It was a dollar drain that was viewed with interest by the Chancellor of the Exchequer. Rumours arose of special taxes that were likely to be imposed on American films and the figure of 25 per cent was mentioned. J. Arthur Rank was in America attempting to set up distribution deals for his films when he heard what was going on in Whitehall. He hurried back and sought an audience with Sir Stafford Cripps, then the President of the Board of Trade, and known to be the decisive voice in matters of taxation, even though the Chancellor at the time was Hugh Dalton. Rank wanted to convey to Cripps that an import tax might save a little in money in the short term, but would lose vastly more in goodwill. Unfortunately, the Minister had a prior engagement and could not see him. Then Rank received word from New York that in order to help the difficult British situation, American producers would agree to freeze part of their dollar earnings and divert them into British production. It seemed a reasonable enough solution. Astonishingly, it proved unacceptable to the Labour government.

Instead, the Chancellor rushed into effect an *ad valorem* duty of 75 per cent, three times that which had been expected, on all films from the dollar area. Moreover the tax was to be based on estimated earnings and to be paid in advance. The outcome was immediate and drastic. The Motion Picture Association of America embargoed all new Hollywood films from entering Britain. The government was amazed by the extreme reaction. One theory suggests that Dalton had expected counter-negotiations, and that the Americans would offer to freeze a higher proportion of their earnings than they had previously suggested. But instead they were playing it as tough and as hard as possible, in the belief that the British public, denied access to new films, would force the government to reconsider. There were, however, voices in Parliament suggesting that without American competition with its superior values, British films now stood a real chance domestically and that Mr Rank had a golden opportunity before him.

But Rank thought otherwise. He was suffering a double shock. His two circuits were now starved of the latest American films, and the painstaking arrangements he had made in the States for the distribution of his own films were now cancelled. Moreover, his credibility there was severely damaged. Americans, used to a system in which the Federal government takes frequent soundings of industry before embarking on controversial legislation, could not believe that the craggy Englishman had had no inkling of what was afoot, and they felt that he had double-crossed them.

And now the British government, having placed Rank in a dismal position, urged him to extricate himself and the British film industry, by instituting a production programme to fill the void left by the American films. In November 1947 Rank announced an investment programme of £9,250,000 to make 47 films, many of them at Pinewood. To raise this kind of money meant an enormous upheaval of the Rank interests. Shareholders of Odeon Theatres, used to the steady dividends from the exhibition side of the industry, suddenly found that they were expected to be involved in the riskier area of production. Odeon was a public company with published accounts, but the umbrella company formed by Rank years earlier, General Cinema Finance Corporation, which hitherto had looked after the production interests, was private and therefore could keep its dealings secret. In 1937 a pledge had been given to Odeon shareholders that they would never be expected to participate in film production. Rank now claimed that he had the approval of 90 per cent of the ordinary shareholders to the new proposal. His own shares were to be sold at par, and this suggestion also aroused so much criticism that in the end he agreed not to touch some £650,000 due to him from Odeon for a period of five years, in effect giving the company an interest-free loan. The Press was gunning for Rank, not merely the left-wing newspapers, but more particularly the *Daily Express* and the *Financial Times*, and the complexity of the various business interests generated hostility and suspicion.

The next move was to effect a merger of the Odeon and Gaumont circuits, which was again seen as a violation of pledges given earlier. The government yielded to the arguments that centralised management would reduce inefficiency, although they asked that programming still remain separate, so that Odeons could not play Gaumont releases and vice-versa, a condition that to some extent removed the reason for the merger, which was to strengthen booking power.

It was increasingly clear that the *ad valorem* tax had been a disaster. It had not even stopped the dollar drain, since not only were there 125 new American films stockpiled, but there was a great spate of reissues, and the duty could not be made retroactive. Moreover, the gestation period of a film, rather like a baby, is usually around nine months, and so Rank was unable to fill the gap overnight. In March 1948, Harold Wilson, the new President of the Board of Trade (Cripps was by now Chancellor, the luckless Dalton having resigned over a budget leak) and Eric Johnston, representing the Motion Picture Association of America, reached agreement for the repeal of the tax, which was to take effect in May. It was to be replaced by a scheme whereby the Americans would be allowed to take out $17 million a year, for two years, a figure that could be increased by the equivalent of the earnings on British films in the States. The balance of American earnings was to be used in various ways inside and outside the industry. It was thought that $33 million would be saved by this new proposal, a great deal more than through the former ill-conceived tax. Then, almost before the ink was dry, the government hurled another blow at the Americans, which was to have serious repercussions on the British film industry. In the new Cinematograph Films Act of 1948 they raised the quota to a massive 45 per cent.

Yet again Rank was accused of calumny. And now he was on the brink of disaster. Harold Wilson was partly to blame for what happened next. He had failed to take into account what would happen when the Hollywood embargo was lifted. He should have insisted on a phased release of unscreened American films, but instead he laid down no conditions and there was a flood. Many of the new, long-awaited films such as *Gentlemen's Agreement, Sitting Pretty, Body and Soul, The Naked City* and *The Bishop's Wife* were powerful box-office attractions and Rank, whose own pictures under the 1948 programme were only just becoming available, had to watch helplessly as the cinemagoers demonstrated their preference for Hollywood. The Rank debts piled up. By October £13½ million was owed to the National Provincial Bank. In the following year it was over £16 million. It looked very much as if film production would be suspended altogether.

Pinewood had been in the vanguard of the film programme. The most adventurous concept of the time had been Independent Frame, a system of ambitious production pre-planning devised by David Rawnsley, who was the head of the Rank Film Research Department. He had conceived the idea during the war when studio space had been very tight, and Rank had

been prepared to invest in the system when production resumed after the war at Pinewood. Basically, it meant that instead of the shooting progressing from stage to stage, so that while one scene was being shot on one set carpenters and plasterers were at work building another, stages would be so designed that sets could be wheeled in and installed when they were needed, and time need never be wasted while such sets were built. To make the sets mobile an elaborate series of rostrums, which could be adjusted to various heights and angles, were provided. Scenery, however, became minimal. Backgrounds were mostly to be provided by back projection and special screen holders were made, together with a huge projection tower with lights which could be positioned automatically. There was also a mobile spot rail that could move arcs 180 degrees.

It was found that even interiors could largely be provided by projection techniques. Actors might be performing in what looked like a real room, but apart from perhaps a table, chair and door the rest would all be photographic background. It even proved unnecessary to send the stars on location. Any exteriors could be shot in long-shot with stand-ins, and the rest could be organised in the studio with the back projection plates made on location.

There was one serious disadvantage to the system. In order to be properly effective an enormous amount of pre-planning had to go into a film. The blocking of the actors' movements had to be worked out on paper and in constant rehearsal, long before the cameras started to turn. While some directors like to work that way, many do not, and their inspirational juices only begin to flow on the set. Actors, too, quite often prefer the tangible to the abstract, and their movements within the Independent Frame required total precision within a void, and a need for concentration beyond that previously expected. The unions also saw the abandonment of their traditional methods as a serious threat to livelihoods, although they were, in any case, in serious jeopardy.

In order to give the director an immediate view of his scenes Rawnsley also devised the Cyclops eye, a television camera linked to the film camera, providing instant 'rushes' at the moment of shooting. Television was still a very infant medium, and this device was way ahead of its time. There was no videotape in those days to provide a playback, which would have been much more useful. But the Cyclops eye indicated the direction of his thinking. After a few Independent Frame films the system was quietly dropped—though not until £600,000 had been spent. Because many of the techniques were similar to those later used in television studios, there was a

Anne Vernon in *Warning to Wantons*,
a star imported specially from France

Gordon Jackson and Sally Ann Howes in
Stop Press Girl, so silly it was withdrawn
after a critics' mauling

substantial technical legacy left to Pinewood. For instance, the standards of
back projection of film and slide have since always been higher there than
in the rest of the world's studios. And the Pinewood travelling-matte, in
which actors could be rephotographed against a moving background, was
another device that greatly influenced future film and television production.
When Independent Frame was given up (although there are still many
visible traces of it around Pinewood such as the scenery rostrums) the need
had passed to make full economic use of studio space; instead, the problem
was to finance enough films to keep it occupied at all.

The few Independent Frame films that were made were produced by
Donald Wilson, who also directed the first, *Warning to Wantons,* a stagey
comedy starring the French actress Anne Vernon. A much better
attempt was *Floodtide,* directed by Frederick Wilson and featuring a young
Gordon Jackson, which with its settings on Clydeside and extensive location footage had a more realistic atmosphere. *Stop Press Girl,* with Sally
Ann Howes, was a disaster, a misfired comedy savaged by the critics and
ignored by the public. *Poet's Pub,* an adaptation of Eric Linklater's novel,
also failed to generate much excitement, and although Sydney Box of
Gainsborough employed the system in Montgomery Tully's *Boys in Brown,*
a Borstal story from a play by William Douglas Home, it was during the
shooting of *Prelude to Fame,* directed by Fergus McDonnell in which
Jeremy Spenser played an exploited musical prodigy, that the decision was
taken to call a halt on further development.

Things were none too happy on other fronts. Independent Producers
was breaking up. That other giant of British films, Alexander Korda, had
re-established London Films at Shepperton and had somehow survived the
financial débâcle of three ponderous and costly films, *Anna Karenina, An
Ideal Husband* and *Bonnie Prince Charlie.* He lured Rank's major director,
Carol Reed, who had left even before his last Rank film, the widely-
acclaimed *Odd Man Out,* had been released. There had been disagreements
over the budget, which had been exceeded by a third. Now Korda was
after more of Rank's stable. Korda and Rank were often apparently at the

Right: Richard Attenborough and Jack
Warner in *Boys in Brown*
Below: John Blythe, Dirk Bogarde, Michael
Medwin and Richard Attenborough in
stir with the potatoes

Sally Gray in *Obsession*, directed at
Pinewood by Edward Dmytryk, exiled
from Hollywood

opposite ends of a seesaw—when one was up the other was down. Exploiting Rank's difficulties, Korda made attractive offers to his other film-makers who had been receiving lectures on spending too much money. Michael Powell and Emeric Pressburger, in hot water over the cost of *The Red Shoes*—although time was to vindicate them, for no Rank film was to earn so much in America for many years—were persuaded by Korda to leave and they did, to make *The Small Back Room*. Next Launder and Gilliat, who had recently been responsible for *London Belongs to Me*, from a Norman Collins novel with Richard Attenborough as a small-time South London murderer, came under attack at Rank. Their last film had been their most ambitious, *The Blue Lagoon*, from the H. de Vere Stacpoole novel about two children growing up on a tropical island. The end result in spite of Technicolor was dull, and yet it was the most successful picture that the pair had made with Rank, in terms of box-office. They left because they felt the interference and control that had been blissfully lacking when Independent Producers was set up, was now crippling the output.

Next to quit was the Ian Dalrymple-Wessex team. It had made *Once a Jolly Swagman*, a film with a speedway setting, directed by Jack Lee, and *All Over the Town*, a story about a seaside local newspaper, directed by Derek Twist. During the shooting of Thorton Freeland's *Dear Mr Prohack*, a screen version of Arnold Bennett's novel, with Cecil Parker, Glynis Johns, Dirk Bogarde and Hermione Baddeley, it was agreed that it would be the last Wessex film to be made at Pinewood. Needless to say, it turned out to be the best.

Even the talented Cineguild group could survive no longer. David Lean dissipated a lot of his energy directing his future wife Ann Todd in his most tedious film, *The Passionate Friends*, a bloodless adaptation of an H. G. Wells story. Originally Ronald Neame was to have directed it, but relations proved impossible and he left. Lean then made another flop, *Madeleine*, with Ann Todd, a slow-moving narrative of the true story of a girl tried for the murder of her lover in mid-Victorian Glasgow. Lean left to join Korda. Meanwhile, Anthony Havelock-Allan, who had produced the most successful of the Cineguild films, had left to set up his own production company which would release through British Lion, now controlled by Korda.

Part of the Korda success had been brought about by his ability to prise money from normally tightly-clenched hands. Before the war he had extracted fortunes from the City, and particularly Prudential Assurance. Now, with Rank against the wall, he was to get a gigantic £3 million loan from the government itself. What had happened was that some four years after the recommendation of the wartime Palache Committee, the National

Left: Richard Attenborough as Percy Boon sees a report on the murder he has committed in *London Belongs to Me*
Below: Richard Attenborough is interrogated by detectives—a Pinewood outdoor set representing South London, by Roy Oxley

Above: Dirk Bogarde as a successful
speedway rider talks to his mechanic
(Dudley Jones) in *Once a Jolly Swagman*
Below: Cecil Parker and Hermione Baddeley

Film Finance Corporation had been established, giving the state tentative participation in the industry. Palache had also recommended a government-owned renting organisation, but this proposal was not implemented. Harold Wilson, the minister responsible for the film industry, as President of the Board of Trade, announced the formation of the new corporation which would have £5 million of taxpayers' money at its disposal and was to be linked to an established renter. Somewhat surprisingly, Wilson was insisting that monies for production from this new source would have to be channelled through the distribution side of the industry, rather than be directly placed in the hands of the producers. Rank refused an offer of government money, preferring to cut back production rather than increase his borrowings any further. Korda, on the other hand, accepted first a £2 million loan for his British Lion Corporation, and as the sum proved to be inadequate to get his production programme under way had it topped up to £3 million. The £2 million balance was to go to independent groups. The first managing director of the NFFC, James Lawrie, had to work pragmatically in the

David Lean (in dark overcoat) directs
Ann Todd on location in Hyde Park for
The Passionate Friends

Editing *Chitty Chitty Bang Bang*. Note
"squeezed" anamorphic image on film

Pinewood's biggest-ever set—inside the
volcano in *You Only Live Twice*

Bryan Forbes in *All Over The Town* with
Sandra Dorne

strange jungle of the film industry, assessing the merits of all the applicants
for finance, and in view of the fact that he had had virtually no previous
experience in the field, he did surprisingly well. Within a year or two of its
inception the NFFC could point to the successes of such films as Carol
Reed's *The Third Man*, Ian Dalrymple and Jack Lee's *The Wooden Horse*,
Launder and Gilliat's *The Happiest Days of Your Life* and *State Secret* as
happy examples of sound investment—all films by former Rank men. But
initially money was lost, and the nature of the NFFC's brief meant that
there was no place for the adventurous and experimental production—the
possibility of commercial success had to be the major criterion for a loan.

At the end of 1948 Wilson had also established not one, but two commit-
tees of inquiry into the film industry. The committee under Sir Arnold
Plant looked into the distribution and exhibition side, while the working
party under Sir George Gater was to examine financing and ways of cutting
production costs. Although they were both handicapped by the tightness
of their respective terms of reference, which inevitably overlapped each
other, and by the lamentable statistical evidence available for reference (at
that time there was not even an aggregate of the numbers and capacity of
British cinemas on file at the Board of Trade) they were able to make
positive recommendations. Both complained about the excessive Entertainments Tax which seemed particularly heavy for cinemas. For instance,
in 1950 out of gross receipts in British cinemas of £105 million, the tax
took nearly £37 million, or 35 per cent of the total. The amount left to the
producers that year was about 15 per cent. The tax had been started as a
temporary measure during the First World War in order to boost the war

Ivan Desny watches Ann Todd dance
with Norman Wooland in David Lean's
Madeleine

effort. It was an excellent example of the Treasury's reluctance to give up a tax even when the need for it had passed and the industry on which it was levied was being bled into extinction. Rank joined the fight to lessen the tax burden, but it was to be several years before any substantial relief was forthcoming, by which time irrevocable damage had been done.

Before then, however, the government did establish the British Film Production Fund, which was to take its name after the Second Secretary of the Treasury, Sir Wilfred Eady, who was the author of the plan. It was to work in the form of a levy on takings after a proportion of tax had been removed, with total abolition on the cheapest seats. The idea was to get some money back into the industry for distribution on, to quote Mr Wilson, 'a purely automatic and objective basis'. It could immediately be seen that the primary benefits of Eady money would go to the successful, rather than the unsuccessful, which seemed to some extent to negate its worthy purpose, but with various adjustments over the years Eady has proved an immensely valuable element of British film financing. One of its aspects was the setting aside of a small percentage for worthwhile projects, the most notable of which was the establishment of the Children's Film Foundation. Among the philanthropic enterprises of J. Arthur Rank in the optimistic years had been the group devoted to making good features for children's programmes, notably at the Saturday morning cinema clubs, but with retrenchment that division had to be closed down. Now it could be re-established. Mary Field, who had run the Rank Children's Films division, was put in charge, and Rank was made chairman.

Another welcome move was the lowering of the quota from the ridiculous figure of 45 per cent to a more realistic 30 per cent. But a new and alarming portent of what was to come began to be apparent. The summer of 1949 was exceptionally fine and audiences were thin. In December of that year the first provincial television station was opened at Sutton Coldfield to serve Birmingham and the Midlands. From now on television was no longer limited to a small London coterie, and it was only a matter of time before the whole country would be within its range. The number of licences for domestic sets had gone from 14,000 in 1947 in the first year of television after the war to 343,000 in 1950, but henceforth the increase was to be in millions.

5 The Haul Back

A T THE end of the 'forties the Rank empire was in shreds. Production at Pinewood and the other studios was severely curtailed. David Hand's expensive animation unit at Cookham was wound up. *This Modern Age*, the monthly news magazine which had in its short life gained much prestige, was stopped. Independent Frame was abandoned. The Children's films ended. Highbury Studios closed, and with them vanished the Company of Youth. Rank's overdraft with the National Provincial Bank was over £16 million and drastic measures were the only answer.

But there was a man of the hour. John Davis, the City accountant who had joined Rank in 1939 to sort out the Odeon finances, and managing director since 1948, now emerged as the executive with a head cool enough to contemplate the ruins and pull something out of them. It was a survival course to the top, and there were many casualties. The extravagant Filippo del Giudice had already fallen to Davis. Sydney Box of Gainsborough was sent on a year's holiday. The Gainsborough Studios at Islington and Shepherd's Bush were closed, the latter being sold to the BBC, who still use it. George Archibald (later Lord Archibald), who had been in control of Independent Producers at Pinewood, also left. At Denham Studios, production had been in the hands of Joseph Somlo and Earl St John. Now Somlo left. Effectively, the Denham era was at an end—only a part of the studio leased to Twentieth Century-Fox remained open for a short time. Production was now to be concentrated at Pinewood Studios under the control of Earl St John, the man who had run the Paramount circuit before the war, and who could be assumed to have some idea of what constituted good box office.

Davis then slashed production budgets. In future £150,000 was to be the upper limit, and no film was to be contemplated that went over the top. The company that took over the management of the studios and serviced the three companies now grouped there, Pinewood Films, Two Cities and Gainsborough, was called J. Arthur Rank Productions Ltd. There were many departures from the Organisation, some with generous golden hand-shakes after many years of service. Davis believed in streamlining, and was

Kenneth More and Trevor Howard in the
Betty Box/Ralph Thomas production of
The Clouded Yellow

Above: Wilfrid Hyde-White confers with
Michael Redgrave in *The Browning Version*

Below: Nigel Patrick, Michael Redgrave
and Jean Kent, the triangle of *The
Browning Version*

anxious to get straightforward, popular films into the cinemas, with fewer costly experiments. Executives who stayed now faced a 10 per cent cut in their salaries, an unwelcome measure at a time of steady inflation.

There were one or two portents to the good in this period of austere gloom. Korda may have gained most of the talented directors who had worked at Pinewood in the 'forties, but Anthony Asquith now returned to the fold, with his own company, Javelin Films, which had as its chairman Lord Grantley, the former managing director of the Studios. Asquith also had a link with Earl St John, who as manager of the Plaza, Piccadilly Circus, a Paramount cinema, had given Asquith his first film booking, when he played *Shooting Stars* in 1928. The initial film under the new programme was *The Woman in Question*, a tightly budgeted and somewhat disappointing work in which Jean Kent portrayed a murdered woman seen through the eyes of several people, but he followed it with a sensitive, carefully observed adaptation of Terence Rattigan's one-act play, *The Browning Version*, in which Michael Redgrave played a cuckolded classics

Anouk Aimée, Herbert Lom and Trevor Howard in *The Golden Salamander*

Joan Greenwood, Michael Redgrave and
Michael Denison in *The Importance of
Being Earnest*

master, Jean Kent a flashy, faithless wife and Nigel Patrick her lover. The
atmosphere of public school life and Redgrave's performance as a failed
schoolmaster gave the film great distinction. Asquith's next was also a
triumph for the studios in which it was made, *The Importance of Being
Ernest*, in which the definitive Lady Bracknell of Edith Evans was pre-
served on film for the eternal delight of posterity. He went on to make *The
Final Test* and the less satisfactory aviation film, *The Net*, at Pinewood.

The government had encouraged American producers to film in England
and eventually Pinewood was to benefit, with Disney filming *The Sword and
the Rose* with Richard Todd there. There had been several earlier films at
other studios which had been American co-productions, notably *The
Mudlark* made by Twentieth Century-Fox at Denham, which was selected
for the Royal Film Performance of 1950, and Disney's *Treasure Island*, the
first of many Disney pictures made in Britain.

Meanwhile, however, Pinewood had drawn in its horns and the new
diminished production schedule had a few excitements. *The Clouded
Yellow* was a workmanlike pursuit thriller, produced by Betty Box (sister of
Sydney) and directed by Ralph Thomas, a team that was to make a number
of unpretentious, popular films. In this one Jean Simmons ably coped with
the role of a girl under psychological pressure and suspicion of murder,
with Trevor Howard as the amiable hero helping her out of trouble. *White
Corridors*, directed by Pat Jackson, was a hospital drama, anticipating the
tensions of *Emergency Ward-10* which would burst on to the television

Anthony Asquith with Edith Evans, the
definitive Lady Bracknell

airwaves a few years later, while *The Adventurers*, directed by David Macdonald, was set in post-Boer War Africa, with Dennis Price and Jack Hawkins on the trail for diamonds. *Night Without Stars*, directed by Anthony Pelissier, was set in the south of France, with David Farrar as a near-blind British lawyer in love with a girl played by Nadia Gray. More original was *Appointment with Venus*, another film from the Box-Thomas team, in which a commando raid was launched on the German-occupied Channel Islands in order to liberate a prize cow. There were sequels to a successful Gainsborough portmanteau film, *Quartet*, which consisted of

David Niven and Glynis Johns with Venus, in *Appointment with Venus*, target for a wartime commando raid

Right: Margaret Leighton with Noël
Coward between takes for *The Astonished
Heart*
Below: James Hayter and Kathleen
Harrison on location in Brompton Road
for a scene in 'The Verger' episode of *Trio*

Alec Guinness as Arnold Bennett's Denry
Machin and Valerie Hobson in *The Card*

four stories by Somerset Maugham who had been signed up by Anthony
Darnborough, responsible the previous year for getting Noël Coward to
play in and co-direct with Terence Fisher *The Astonished Heart*. At Pinewood were made *Trio* and *Encore*. In one of the stories, *Sanatorium*, in the
former film, an episode directed by Harold French, a sad coincidence
robbed Guy Rolfe of the part eventually played by Michael Rennie, that of
a TB patient convalescing. Rolfe succumbed to TB and had to enter a real
sanatorium. Muriel Box (wife of Sydney) was to direct another Maugham
story, *The Beachcomber*, with Robert Newton, previously filmed under its
original title, *Vessel of Wrath*.

Ronald Neame directed Alec Guinness in a reasonable adaptation of an
Arnold Bennett Five Towns story, *The Card*, in which the hero worked his
way up to become mayor, with Glynis Johns, Valerie Hobson and Petula
Clark as the women who saw him on his way, and Val Guest produced and
directed his wife, Yolande Donlan, in *Penny Princess*, an amusing Technicolor comedy in which a shopgirl inherited a tiny European country.
George Brown produced and Ken Annakin directed Jack Hawkins and
Laya Raki in a saga of the early settling of New Zealand, *The Seekers*.
Hawkins, who had made his first film as long ago as 1930, was already
becoming noted for his war performances and one made at Pinewood at
the time was *The Malta Story*, directed by Brian Desmond Hurst. A few
major American stars were also now making films at Pinewood. Claudette
Colbert had starred with Jack Hawkins and Anthony Steel in Ken Annakin's *The Planter's Wife*, another war story, this time set on a Malayan
rubber plantation. Gregory Peck appeared in Ronald Neame's Technicolor version of Mark Twain's story set in Victorian London, *The Million
Pound Note*, opposite a hitherto unknown actress, Jane Griffith, although

Gregory Peck attired as a toff in *The Million Pound Note*.

Peck returned to Pinewood to make *The Purple Plain*

the result was more bland than satirical. He returned within the year to make *The Purple Plain*, a war story set in Burma and directed by Robert Parrish.

One of the most successful films ever made at Pinewood went into production in 1952. The story of how it came to be made there is told by Michael Balcon in his autobiography, *Michael Balcon Presents . . . A Lifetime of Films*. It seems that Henry Cornelius, the director of *Passport to Pimlico* and *The Galloping Major*, both Ealing comedies, had left to go independent, a rare thing for an Ealing director ever to do. He had worked out an outline with William Rose of a story of a veteran car and a drive to Brighton, ideal material for an Ealing comedy. However, Balcon could see no way of getting Cornelius back into the small Ealing group without breaking up a carefully arranged schedule. Aware that the film could be a winner, Balcon sent Cornelius to Pinewood to see Earl St John, who as it happened was not quite so enthusiastic, but agreed to let the film go ahead, particularly as the National Film Finance Corporation was providing backing. *Genevieve* starred John Gregson and Kenneth More, Dinah Sheridan and Kay Kendall, and two enchanting Edwardian cars. With a musical score played on the mouth organ by Larry Adler and pleasant Technicolor photography with the two vehicles acting as a backdrop to the bickering competitiveness of the two couples, the film quelled earlier doubts by becoming an enormous box-office success, and it can still draw a reasonable audience nearly a quarter-of-a-century later. William Rose, an American who became a naturalised Briton, went on to write more Ealing comedies and, in Hollywood, *Guess Who's Coming to Dinner?* Neither Kay Kendall nor Henry Cornelius were so lucky; both died before the end of the 'fifties.

Genevieve—the most famous Pinewood film of all time. Kay Kendall, Kenneth More, Dinah Sheridan and John Gregson en route for Brighton

The mantle of the Ealing comedies now seemed to be passing westwards into Buckinghamshire, where it was broadening out into a more robust idiom. Ralph Thomas and Betty Box had a huge success with *Doctor in the House*, the first of a series of books by Richard Gordon on the lighter side of medical practice to be brought to the screen. It was a chronicle of the student life, with its japes and rags, binges and exams, performed by a well-chosen cast which included Dirk Bogarde, Kenneth More, Donald Sinden, Kay Kendall and James Robertson Justice, the latter playing an irascible and distinguished surgeon. Its unsubtle jokes such as the famous 'What's the bleeding time?' line would never have been acceptable in the Ealing product, but the popularity of the film inspired a series which was to run spasmodically on into the 'seventies, when television regenerated the characters. The second 'Doctor' film, *Doctor at Sea*, released in 1955, in which the central character, still played by Dirk Bogarde, secured a post as ship's medical officer on a cruise ship, was noteworthy in introducing to British audiences a 21-year-old French actress called Brigitte Bardot.

Kenneth More was to become the number one box-office British star of the 'fifties, and his superb comic timing enhanced many a film in that period. Donald Sinden, who had made his film début in Ealing's *The Cruel Sea* found himself typecast in the buffoonish 'Doctor' role, much to his detriment as a serious actor.

Donald Houston, Donald Sinden,
Kenneth More and Dirk Bogarde in
Doctor in the House

Shirley Ann Field models a Kayser 'baby doll' pyjama set while filming *Seven Thunders*. Still by Cornel Lucas

Judy Carne poses for Ian Jeayes during her film début in *A Pair of Briefs*, directed by Ralph Thomas, produced by Betty Box

Atmospheric Cornel Lucas still from Basil Dearden's thriller *Sapphire*, with Yvonne Buckingham and Harry Baird

Frankie Vaughan and Anne Heywood in *The Heart of a Man* directed by Herbert Wilcox, another Cornel Lucas still

Donald Sinden, Donald Houston, Kenneth
More, Muriel Pavlow and Dirk Bogarde in
Doctor in the House

Joan Sims and Liz Fraser watch James
Robertson Justice carry Eve Eden out of a
raided nightclub in *Doctor in Love*

Medical students have a rag in
Doctor in the House

Norman Wisdom had come to films by way of television, probably the first British comedian of any substance to make his name in that medium first. In 1953 he starred in his first film, directed by John Paddy Carstairs, *Trouble in Store*. The Wisdom character was that of a little man in an ill-fitting suit, battling against the aggravations of a hostile world with infinite good humour and intentions. There was a certain resemblance to Chaplin, and occasional lapses into mawkishness. But with the splendid Jerry Desmonde as a pompous foil (he had been the most celebrated of the great Sid Field's stooges) Wisdom emerged as the most important British screen clown since the pre-war days of Will Hay and George Formby, and henceforth for many years an annual Norman Wisdom film was standard fare from The Rank Organisation.

In the face of the dwindling audience figures as television flourished changes were occurring in film exhibition. The watershed for the growth of television is often thought to be the Coronation of 1953, a lavish ceremonial occasion viewed in several countries as it happened, which seemed to render actuality film extinct. Certainly it sparked off a boom in set buying, and by the end of the year well over three million licences were issued. Plans were also afoot to launch commercial television in Britain. In America the television revolution had really taken hold, and production of feature films was flagging. Showmanship came to the fore. There was a brief attempt to establish three-dimensional films, but as they required special viewing glasses for the audience, and two projectors in simultaneous use, the process was too cumbersome to catch on and was eventually abandoned. Twentieth Century-Fox, however, reintroduced an invention from the 'twenties, the anamorphic lens by which a much wider-shaped scene could be filmed on standard 35mm stock, then 'squeezed' optically to fit the frame. With a similar lens on the projector it could then be shown in the original wide proportions. Called CinemaScope, it produced a screen image that was two-and-a-half times as wide as it was high, and the first

Above: James Robertson Justice faces the camera for *Doctor at Sea*
Left: Brigitte Bardot with Dirk Bogarde in *Doctor at Sea*
Right: The 21-year-old 'French jewel' on loan to Pinewood having made nine films in France

film made this way, *The Robe*, pulled in crowds wherever it was shown. The other companies followed, with one exception.

Paramount devised another system, using a variable ratio, which meant that the final result could be projected on any number of screen shapes, from the standard 'Academy' shape to something approaching the proportions of CinemaScope. In shooting, the film ran horizontally instead of vertically through the camera gate, and the enlarged image was supposed to produce much sharper projection prints. The system was known as VistaVision. For a long time, Paramount remained alone among the American companies using it, the others opting for CinemaScope, or variations of it.

Twentieth Century-Fox saw CinemaScope and stereophonic sound going together. They wanted theatres to wire up for the magnetic multiple soundtrack which needed new amplification and speakers. Exhibitors argued that the full impact was in the image, and their patrons would not care whether the sound, if it was turned up loud enough, was coming from

Ian Carmichael, Peter Finch and Kay
Kendall in *Simon and Laura*

Daisy the alligator terrorizes young starlets
—a George Ward publicity still of the
mid-Fifties

an old optical track or a new 4-track stereophonic magnetic one. Their resources had already been severely strained with the installation of new screens and projection equipment. Rank took the firmest stand of all and announced that no more of their theatres would be wired for stereophonic sound, and as far as production was concerned many of their films would be made in VistaVision. Fox retaliated by taking their films out of Odeon and Gaumont cinemas, and there was even an attempt to create a fourth releasing circuit out of Granada, Essoldo and one or two other independents, an enterprise that failed to make it as there just were not enough theatres. It was two years before a rapprochement was reached and Rank once more began to exhibit Twentieth Century-Fox films. By that time the novelty value of VistaVision had worn thin, and eventually the system

Above: Director Ken Annakin adjusts
Diana Dors' dress for *Value for Money*
Below: Diana Dors at Pinewood in her
sky-blue Cadillac
Left: Trouble with the headdress—Diana
Dors in a bridal veil for *Value for Money*

David Tomlinson gets the worst of it in
All for Mary

was dropped, with CinemaScope and later Panavision being used for productions that required such extra production values.

The Rank films of the 'fifties were often criticised for their blandness, and it is certainly true that there was an emphasis on comedy or simple human problems such as Guy Green's *Lost*, which was about a neurotic woman baby stealer. The usual fare consisted of pictures like *Simon and Laura*, directed by Muriel Box, in which a feuding marital pair (Peter Finch and Kay Kendall) simulated happy marriage in a TV series, J. Lee-Thompson's *An Alligator Named Daisy*, with Diana Dors, in which a songwriter was torn between an heiress, an ordinary girl and his pet reptile, and Wendy Toye's *All For Mary*, a farce about a grown man with a bossy nanny interfering with his love life. Some films were made on money from the NFFC, and as far back as 1951 British Film Makers Ltd had been formed at Pinewood with the intention of taking advantage of this source of finance, reversing the earlier decision by Rank not to be involved with money from a government fund. In 1953 Group Film Productions Ltd took over British Film Makers and the NFFC no longer had any participation, and in 1955 the name was changed to The Rank Organisation Film Productions Ltd. In the previous year the old company D & P Studios Ltd, which owned Pinewood, went into liquidation and the parent company, British and Dominions, took over.

Earl St John, the production chief at Pinewood from 1951, was a notable showman, born in Baton Rouge, Louisiana. After military service in Europe during the First World War he decided to stay. By 1924 he was an independent exhibitor in Manchester, running the Ardwick Green Picture House. He then got a job as head of exploitation at Paramount in London, his first assignments being to promote *The Ten Commandments* and *The Covered Wagon*. In 1926 he opened the Plaza and started the Paramount circuit which was bought by Odeon twelve years later. John Davis made him his personal assistant in 1939 and, after the war, joint managing director of Two Cities at Denham. After becoming executive producer at Pinewood the stamp on output was mostly his. Norman Wisdom, spotted in a 15-minute act in a television programme, was St John's proudest discovery. If anyone suggested in his presence that it might be a fine day, he had only one retort. 'I hope it rains like blazes.'

Unfortunately, that was not what it was doing. The audience slide continued, inexorably. John Davis had performed a financial miracle, lopping more than £3 million of the £16 million Rank overdraft in the first year of his reign, and by the mid-'fifties reducing it to a mere £4 million, a healthy enough level with which to stay in business. But while there had been 1585 million admissions to Britain's cinemas in 1945, by 1957 the number had shrunk to only 915 million. Rises in admission prices had slightly compensated, although net takings in 1957 were down to £65 million, as opposed to the peak year of 1946 when they were £76 million. Entertainments tax

John Gregson in *The Battle of the River Plate*, the story of the attack and scuttling of the pocket battleship *Graf Spee*

Kenneth More as Douglas Bader, the
legless RAF ace, sasses the krauts in
Reach for the Sky
Above: Trying out his tin legs

Olivier with Marilyn Monroe for
The Prince and the Showgirl, her only
film outside Hollywood

Laurence Olivier with Dame Sybil
Thorndike in *The Prince and the Showgirl*

was still removing more than a quarter of the gross but in the 1957 Cinematograph Films Act the means were provided for its progressive reduction
with total abolition in 1960, thus ending an impost on the cinema clamped
on it during the darkest days of the Great War. The campaign for abolition
had taken many years, and films were the last public amusements to be
subject to the tax.

The Rank group also began to close down the most unprofitable of its
theatres in the mid-'fifties. At that time the policy was to shut and not sell
to other operators, so cinemas became supermarkets and garages, factories
and building sites—the latter often the most attractive proposition to the
owners, as they often stood on prime town-centre sites which had soared
in value since they were acquired. By 1958 the Odeon and Gaumont
circuits had been so thinned out that they could be merged into one Rank
circuit without public outcry.

In 1955 commercial television began in London and in the following
year spread to the Midlands and North. By 1957 there were nearly seven
million TV licences issued, and now feature films, albeit elderly ones, were
beginning to be seen with regularity over the air. ITV had acquired a large
Korda package and the BBC some 100 films from the RKO library. In the
teeth of this competition the film industry was in for a hard fight, and the
Pinewood stages were one of the principal battlegrounds. War films,
curiously, were having a vogueish success at the time, and stories of gritty
endurance, such as Lewis Gilbert's *Reach for the Sky*, with Kenneth More
creditably portraying the legless ace, Douglas Bader, Jack Lee's *A Town
Like Alice* from the Nevil Shute novel about the Japanese invasion of

Malaya, and Michael Powell and Emeric Pressburger's return engagement at Pinewood, *The Battle of the River Plate*, about the siege and scuttling of the Graf Spee, all had commercial success as well as being worthy pictures. Norman Wisdom was also to be relied on to bring in an audience, and his films with John Paddy Carstairs directing, *One Good Turn*, *Man of the Moment*, *Up in the World*, *Just My Luck* and so on, looked to be an annual bout of his comic skills.

In 1956 Pinewood attracted world headlines when Marilyn Monroe journeyed there to make her only film outside Hollywood, with Laurence Olivier playing opposite her as well as directing. It was *The Prince and the Showgirl*, from a play by Terence Rattigan, a curious choice for Olivier, fresh from his cinematic Shakespearean triumph, *Richard III*. Monroe's performance was far from plastic and artificial, but sweetly knowing, and counterpointed his stiff, aloof approach as an infatuated Ruritanian prince in London for the 1911 Coronation. Two other Hollywood stars were at Pinewood in the same year, filming *The Iron Petticoat*, an unsuccessful

Norman Wisdom, the mainstay of Rank
screen comedy, in *Up in the World*, with
Michael Ward

Lord Rank, assisted by his star, Anne Heywood cuts the cake at the 21st birthday celebration, 30 September 1957

variation on the Ninotchka theme. They were Katharine Hepburn and Bob Hope.

Pinewood celebrated its 21st anniversary on 30 September 1957 with a huge lunch for 500 guests, in a big marquee. There was a birthday cake, presentations to Lord and Lady Rank (he had been ennobled in Pinewood's 21st year) and Mr and Mrs John Davis, from 21 girls aged 21. There were speakers, including Dirk Bogarde 'as the oldest living member of the contract artists', Lord Rank, John Davis, and the Hon. George Drew, High Commissioner for Canada. Of the four of the original board of directors still connected with the studios, only Ronald Crammond was unable to be there owing to ill health. The others, Spencer Reis, who had been managing director since 1941, W. H. Cockburn and Rank himself were all present. John Davis pointed out that in 1957 Pinewood had produced 18 films, that in the following year the number would be 20, and he announced a £5 million programme.

The guests then went on a guided tour of the studios and gawped in wonder at such sights as the travelling-matte demonstration, special effects, plasterers' and carpenters' shops, and actors such as Cecil Parker strolling around in period costume. The tour of the lot was carefully organised so that none of the German guests would see the replica of part of the infamous Ravensbruck concentration camp that had been erected for a sequence in *Carve Her Name with Pride*.

6 Pinewood Carries On

CERTAINLY in that anniversary year, 1957, there was a large number of films in production at Pinewood. It was a heyday for Dirk Bogarde —he was going straight from one film into another. An intelligent and sensitive actor, his skills at redeeming an inadequate script or injecting depth into a good one were at least recognised by the public, with whom he had considerable box-office power. He made *The Spanish Gardener*, directed by Philip Leacock, then *Ill Met by Moonlight*, a Powell and Pressburger war film, followed by *Doctor at Large*, another in the Box–Thomas series, then *Campbell's Kingdom* by the same team, this time an adventure story set in Canada, and also their version of *A Tale of Two Cities*, playing Sidney Carton, which they followed up with a war film set in Burma, *The Wind Cannot Read*.

The Australian actor Peter Finch was impressive in Jack Lee's *Robbery Under Arms*, a kind of Empire Western, set in the Australian outback of the mid-nineteenth century. Roy Baker made a war film with Hardy Kruger as a German pilot who managed to escape from British hands (a reversal of the usual cliché) called *The One That Got Away*. Hugo Fregonese made a war film with Stephen Boyd and Tony Wright, set in Marseilles, *Seven Thunders*, while *Windom's Way*, directed by Ronald Neame, with Peter Finch and Mary Ure, had a background of the troubles in Malaya, and a screenplay by Jill Craigie, wife of the Labour politician, Michael Foot. *Dangerous Exile*, with Louis Jourdan and Belinda Lee, was a period piece directed by Brian Desmond Hurst, set in the Napoleonic Wars, and *The Gypsy and the Gentleman*, with Melina Mercouri and Keith Michell, a Regency melodrama, represented a curious choice of subject for Joseph Losey, who had earlier in the 'fifties been making films in Britain under different pseudonyms, following his banishment from Hollywood in the McCarthy era. It was a varied list, although clearly and deliberately aimed at the middle of the market.

For during this period John Davis was taking a very close interest in the production programme. His role was always controversial, some regarding

Lord Rank and John Davis stroll through
the streets of revolutionary Paris with
The Tale of Two Cities star, Dirk Bogarde

Top: *Ill Met by Moonlight*, Michael Powell's story of Cretan kidnapping in wartime, with Dirk Bogarde

Centre: Dirk Bogarde in *The Wind Cannot Read* with Michael Medwin
Below: Dirk Bogarde with Ralph Thomas (left) and Betty Box (extreme right) during shooting of *Campbell's Kingdom*

Kenneth More clings on for grim death in
The Thirty Nine Steps

Dirk Bogarde in *The Singer Not the Song*

Kenneth More and Lauren Bacall relax on
location in the 114°F heat of Jaipur during
filming of *North West Frontier*

his judgement as to what constituted a cinematic story highly fallible, others welcoming his cautious approach. As The Rank Organisation became directly responsible for fewer and fewer films, and more and more outside producers were encouraged to lease Pinewood's studio space, it was suggested that Davis 'combines the appearance of taking a risk with the certainty of making a profit'. It was certainly true that to the trained accountant's mind of John Davis, films could only be justified if they provided a healthy return on investment. Under his encouragement The Rank Organisation diversified into many other fields, occasionally with spectacular success such as copying machines—the early deal with Xerox has kept the flag flying on more than one occasion—and sometimes disastrously, as with records. Bingo, hotels, bowling alleys, electronics, hi-fi equipment, motorway service areas and commercial television were just a few of the non-cinema interests that turned The Rank Organisation into a sizeable conglomerate, and inevitably films, with their low yield and precarious foundations, became less of a preoccupation at 38 South Street, the corporate Mayfair headquarters. In the ten years from the time when Davis took control of a company which was £16 million in the red, he had turned it about face, and the 1960 profits were over £7 million. But it certainly was not films that had brought the change of fortune, and had it not been for the strict financial control exercised over the studios and the cinemas, and the diversification, The Rank Organisation would have collapsed.

To emphasise the precarious balance of the film industry and its dwindling audiences, crisis came relatively hard on the heels of Pinewood's 21st anniversary. It is one of the reasons why the festivities of the occasion are not recalled with any great pangs of nostalgia by John Davis. Three months later, some 300 of the Pinewood workers had to be laid off following the cancellation or postponement of four films which were to have cost £1 million. The situation at Britain's other studios was just as grim.

One of the saddest casualties in the retrenchment of the 'fifties was Ealing. Although Michael Balcon had enjoyed a privileged autonomy within The Rank Organisation, which released the films but did not run the studios, there were the inevitable cash problems and severely limited capital resources. Their studio site was in a residential area, and the only change of use acceptable to the local authority was redevelopment for housing. After talks with John Davis, Balcon and his partner, Reg Baker, had agreed that if a suitable offer for Ealing Studios came along it would be better to sell up and transfer production to Pinewood. In 1955 Ealing got such an offer from the BBC who wanted to purchase the studios for the

Dirk Bogarde goes to the guillotine as
Sidney Carton in *The Tale of Two Cities*

Top: Hardy Kruger is captured after
crash-landing in England. Later he will be
The One That Got Away
Right: Donald Sinden takes a breather
while his ancient car is fixed in
Rockets Galore, made on location in the
Outer Hebrides

Melina Mercouri awaits her scene in Joseph Losey's *The Gypsy and the Gentleman*

Above: *The Captain's Table*—the cast steps forward
Left: *The Captain's Table* with John Gregson at its head, then clockwise Peggy Cummins, John Warner, June Jago, Maurice Denham, Nova Nicholson, Nicholas Phipps, Rosalie Ashley, Bill Kerr and Nadia Gray

Norman Wisdom is *Up in the World*
as a window cleaner

ever-expanding television service. So Ealing was sold for little more than
£300,000 and its loan from the National Film Finance Corporation paid
off. In one of the earlier conversations with John Davis Balcon had under-
stood him to say 'I will build two additional stages *for you* at Pinewood.'
It was certainly true that the intention of building two new stages was firm,
but they would not have been for Balcon's exclusive use, it being argued
that Pinewood could not operate on such a basis. Balcon feared that without
the independence which these two stages would have provided the unique
qualities of Ealing would be submerged in the general Rank output. Baker,
however, held a more moderate view and was urged by Davis to use his
influence to win Balcon over. But Balcon remained adamant, and with the
completion of the last true Ealing film, *The Long Arm*, with Jack Hawkins,
the arrangements for financing and distribution by Rank were terminated.
Balcon resigned his seat on the Rank Board, and eventually signed a deal
with M-G-M who allocated a special block for Ealing at their Borehamwood studios. They made some half-dozen films there in the next three
years until the Ealing assets were bought out by Associated British Picture
Corporation, who had no interest in the Ealing name being perpetuated in
production.

Pinewood saw out the 'fifties with many films still made by Rank,
although the independents were now forming a larger proportion. These
latter days of Rank production included comedies such as Norman Wisdom's *The Square Peg* and *Follow a Star*, Mario Zampi's *Too Many Crooks*,
with Terry-Thomas and Bernard Bresslaw, Jack Lee's *The Captain's
Table*, from a Richard Gordon novel, and starring John Gregson, *Rockets*

Above: Stanley Baker as a detective
sergeant shot in Liverpool in
Violent Playground
Right: Howard Keel, an escaped convict,
has saved Anne Heywood from drowning,
in *Floods of Fear*

Galore, directed by Basil Dearden from a Compton Mackenzie novel in a similar vein to his earlier work filmed by Ealing, *Whisky Galore*. The more serious Rank films had included Michael Relph and Basil Dearden's *Violent Playground*, a Liverpool juvenile delinquent story with David McCallum, Philip Leacock's *Innocent Sinners*, which presented another aspect of the problems of an urban childhood, and Charles Crichton's *Floods of Fear*, curiously set in the United States, with Howard Keel as an escaped convict trapped in a flooded house with a terrified Anne Heywood. But by far the most ambitious Rank production was Roy Baker's *A Night to Remember*, which was the story of the 1912 disaster, the sinking of the *Titanic*. Kenneth More played the gallant second officer, Lightoller, with commendable flair, and one of the Pinewood indoor tanks was used as never before. There was also an excellent replica of the doomed ship created by the Studios' set builders. For a Kenneth More film the following year, Twentieth Century-Fox's *Sink the Bismarck!* which was directed by Lewis Gilbert, a new and magnificent outdoor tank was constructed, one of Pinewood's most-valued assets. Kenneth More also co-starred with Lauren Bacall in *North West Frontier*, directed by J. Lee-Thompson. Less well-conceived, perhaps, was the Betty Box-Ralph Thomas remake of Buchan's *The Thirty-Nine Steps*, this time with Kenneth More as Richard Hannay and Taina Elg as the woman he meets on his flight and somehow becomes handcuffed to, an invention of Hitchcock, not Buchan. It was perhaps a mistake to have followed the earlier film version so closely, since it was already some distance from the original.

Among the independents filming at Pinewood and releasing through Rank were Julian Wintle and Leslie Parkyn (Independent Artists) who followed a gauche Cambridge comedy *Bachelor of Hearts*, directed by Wolf Rilla with Hardy Kruger and Sylvia Syms ('A Kraut at Cambridge' might have been a more apt title), with *Never Let Go*, directed by John Guillermin, and *Tiger Bay* (J. Lee-Thompson), with John Mills as a policeman and his younger daughter Hayley making her début on the screen. Her career might well have stopped there, at the age of 12, had Disney not then offered her a contract and whisked her off to Hollywood to be *Pollyanna*.

There had been something of an artistic renaissance in the British cinema at the end of the 'fifties, which in itself was an echo of the shock wave which had reverberated through the theatre in 1956, the year of Suez and *Look Back in Anger*. The film that was regarded as the harbinger of the British equivalent of France's new wave, a movement that had produced Truffaut, Godard and Chabrol, was Jack Clayton's *Room at the Top*, followed by Tony Richardson's screen versions of John Osborne's plays, *Look Back in Anger* and *The Entertainer*, and the Karel Reisz film of Alan

Right: Kenneth More as Commander Lightoller in *A Night to Remember*, the end of the Titanic
Below: Kenneth More in *Sink the Bismarck!*

Above: Kenneth More in action in *North West Frontier*
Below: Kenneth More and Taina Elg in *The Thirty Nine Steps*, a reworking of the famous Hitchcock scene

Bryan Forbes and Richard Attenborough, the team responsible for *Whistle Down the Wind*, and, *opposite*, a scene from the film

Sillitoe's *Saturday Night and Sunday Morning*. Bryan Forbes, for many years a boyish-faced actor and energetic screenwriter, formed a partnership with Richard Attenborough, who had been similarly cursed in the 'fifties with a deceptively youthful countenance, and together they made a film called *The Angry Silence*, a rare attempt at portraying an industrial dispute on the screen. Its modest profit enabled the Forbes-Attenborough team to form Allied Film Makers with Michael Relph and Basil Dearden, and Jack Hawkins and his brother, as the other teams' of partners. Releasing arrangements for their films were made with The Rank Organisation.

The new group had an auspicious start. Bryan Forbes had written a screenplay about a skilfully organised robbery carried out by disgraced ex-Army officers. It was filmed at Pinewood as *The League of Gentlemen*, both Attenborough and Forbes being in it as members of a group led by an efficient Colonel, played by Jack Hawkins. The film had an ironically wry tone, offering a variation on the more usual war story theme, with peacetime criminal intent substituting for a brilliantly executed action against the enemy. The next Allied Film Makers film was far less successful, in spite of having Kenneth More in the lead, and *The Man on the Moon*, screenplay by Relph and Forbes, directed by Dearden, an attempt at an Ealing-type spoof on the British space programme, did not recoup its costs. But there was soon to be consolation in the form of *Whistle Down the Wind*, which Keith Waterhouse and Willis Hall had adapted from a novel by Mary Hayley Bell, the wife of John Mills and mother of Hayley—who returned from Hollywood to take the lead role. She was cast as a little girl on a northern hill farm, who believes that an escaped prisoner found hiding

Jack Hawkins emerges suavely from a
sewer in *The League of Gentlemen*

in a barn is Christ. A beautifully orchestrated study of childhood innocence, reminiscent of René Clément's *Les Jeux Interdits*, it was the first film to be directed by Forbes (after Guy Green, the original choice, had withdrawn to do another film).

Michael Relph and Basil Dearden were helping to push some of the barriers back. They had made *Sapphire*, a thriller which touched on the colour prejudice question, and was noteworthy for its muted Eastmancolor photography. Screenwriter Janet Green wrote with John McCormick the next Allied Film Makers picture, *Victim*, another Relph–Dearden work, which broke another censorship taboo—homosexuality. Dirk Bogarde played a barrister blackmailed by a young homosexual who kills himself when arrested. There followed a moral dilemma; should Bogarde tell all and expose the ring he belongs to, thus ruining his career and marriage, or keep quiet? He chooses the first course. For Bogarde, so long stereotyped in light comedy roles, it was an important step, as well as a courageous one, for the Wolfenden proposals had not at that stage become law, and even

Shirley Ann Field and Kenneth More in
Man in the Moon

Victim: blackmailer (Peter McEnery) and blackmailed (Dirk Bogarde), the first film to examine homosexuality seriously

the word 'queer' had to be defined for provincial audiences. Bogarde discarded one part of his following, the fans of his *Doctor* films, but gained the mien of a serious actor, and paved the way for his later performances in the films of Losey, Schlesinger and Visconti.

Allied Film Makers finally fell apart in 1964, after the failure of Bryan Forbes's excellent *Séance on a Wet Afternoon* to go into profit within a reasonable time. That it made a profit at all was no thanks to the British release, which was partial. The powerful performances of the American actress Kim Stanley as a medium and Richard Attenborough as her timid husband, and the fine line defining sanity and madness were elements of an interesting and creditable work. *Life for Ruth*, a Relph–Dearden film made at Pinewood, with as its subject the religious scruples of a couple whose daughter needs a blood transfusion for her life to be saved, made no impression on the box office at all, and Allied Film Makers suspended film-making owing more than £300,000 to The Rank Organisation. But over the years the money was repaid.

The most publicised and certainly the most expensive débâcle in the history of Pinewood occurred in 1960 when Twentieth Century-Fox embarked on the production of *Cleopatra*. The star was to be Elizabeth Taylor, and from the start it was conceived as a multi-million dollar epic, some sequences using 5000 extras. Massive sets were built on the back lot, and ancient Egypt was recreated under Buckinghamshire skies. But arguments and schisms developed, scripts were discarded, directors replaced.

The ill-fated Cleopatra set on the
Pinewood backlot

Bryan Forbes lines up a scene for *Seance on a Wet Afternoon*—Kim Stanley faces the camera

Eventually shooting commenced, under Joseph L. Mankiewicz, who had also written the final script. Then the biggest disaster of all befell the production. Elizabeth Taylor was stricken with a dangerous, almost mortal illness, and rushed to the London Clinic for a tracheotomy. There was no alternative but to suspend production. The weather was particularly dismal that year and summer rain drizzled all over the monumental sets. Finally, after Elizabeth Taylor's long convalescence the decision was taken to scrap the Pinewood footage and transfer the entire production to Italy, remaking the film from scratch. The Pinewood constructions were pulled down, unused, and that was the end of the biggest film the studios never had. Perhaps Gabriel Pascal, whose earlier Cleopatran spending spree had alienated Rank, was chuckling in heaven. When *Cleopatra* with Taylor, Burton and Rex Harrison finally appeared in 1963 it turned out to be a very dreary work, scarcely justifying its reputation as the most expensive film ever made. Pinewood's *riposte* was the spoof, *Carry on Cleo*, with Amanda Barrie playing the siren of the Nile. Twentieth Century-Fox, aware that their epic would probably not be in the black until the twenty-first century, were not amused and sued over the plagiaristic poster for the latter film.

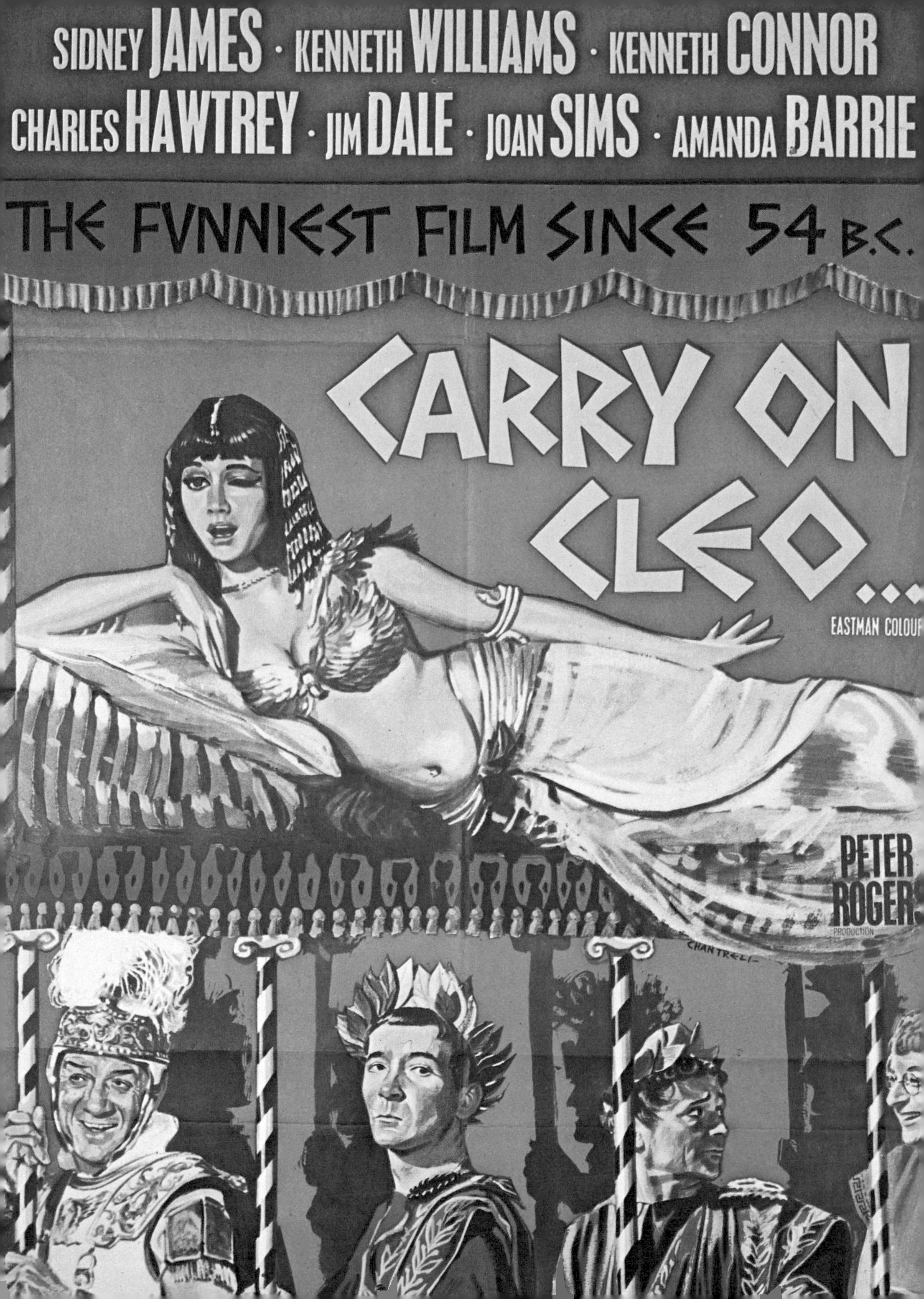
SIDNEY JAMES · KENNETH WILLIAMS · KENNETH CONNOR
CHARLES HAWTREY · JIM DALE · JOAN SIMS · AMANDA BARRIE
THE FUNNIEST FILM SINCE 54 B.C.
CARRY ON CLEO...
EASTMAN COLOUR
PETER ROGERS PRODUCTION
CHANTRELL

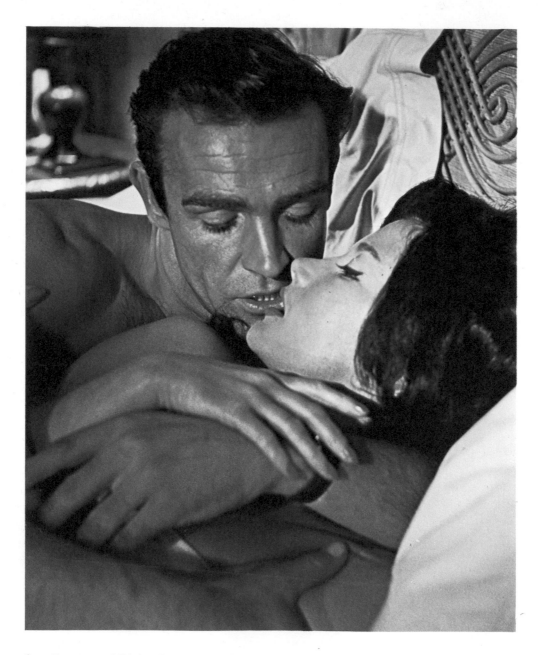

Sean Connery and Eunice Gayson in the first
of the Bond films, *Dr No*

The *Carry On* series, unlike the sad story related above, represents one of Pinewood's most consistent and extraordinary successes. The first film was *Carry on Sergeant* in 1958, a modest, and rather less ribald precursor of the celebrated series, which to date consists of 27 films. The first, like its successors, was directed by Gerald Thomas (brother of Ralph) and produced by Peter Rogers. The full list in order is *Sergeant, Nurse, Teacher, Constable, Regardless, Cruising, Cabby, Jack, Spying, Cleo, Cowboy, Screaming, Follow that Camel, Don't Lose Your Head* (the only two titles not prefixed by *Carry On*), *Doctor, Up the Khyber, Camping, Again Doctor, Loving, Up the Jungle, Henry, At Your Convenience, Matron, Abroad, Girls, Dick, Behind* and the latest, *Carry On England*. Initially, the NFFC backed them but as they were soon seen to be highly profitable Peter Rogers was able to turn to other sources. Perhaps the secret of their continuing success has been their very familiarity. There is a revolving repertory of skilful comic performers, the most notable being Kenneth Williams, the late Sidney James, Hattie Jacques, Kenneth Connor, Barbara Windsor, Charles Hawtrey and Jim Dale, and their gag-laden scripts, usually by Talbot Rothwell, are larded with ancient vulgar jokes and farcical situations (by far the most rewarding area of humorous possibilities has been the hospital —closely followed by holidaying and camping) and there is a predictability of plot. Budgets are so low as to be almost shoestring—the actors exchanging high fees for continuity of employment, the exterior locations usually being somewhere on or adjoining the Pinewood lot. The unpretentious buffoonery of the *Carry On* films, like a celluloid translation of Donald McGill's postcards, with an often obsessive interest in backsides and bosoms, represents a vein of British comedy that is indigenous and enduring, and while not winning awards at film festivals the long-running series has kept the studios active and brought audiences into the cinemas.

But by far the most successful long-running series of films ever made anywhere also emanated from Pinewood Studios. Ian Fleming created his womanising, licensed-to-kill British secret agent, James Bond, in the early 'fifties, but it was nearly ten years and several books later before there was any serious interest in transferring him to the screen. Harry Saltzman, a Canadian-born producer who had backed Woodfall Films and *Look Back in Anger*, had bought options on all the Bond novels except *Casino Royale*, the first one, which Fleming had sold outright in 1955 to Gregory Ratoff for $6000. Saltzman now found that no distributor was willing to guarantee a James Bond picture. Then Albert R. Broccoli, an Italian-American whose family first grew the luscious vegetable bearing the patronymic, and known throughout the industry as 'Cubby', came into the picture. Broccoli was

Carry Ons

MARIE: *Oh come, milord, do you choose to forget that day at Hampton Court?*

CROMWELL: *Hampton?*

MARIE: *When you rescued me from the maze.*

CROMWELL: *Oh yes, when you couldn't find your way out.*

MARIE: *And you couldn't find your way in!*

CROMWELL: *Madam, I beg of you to forget that afternoon. I got carried away.*

MARIE: *Stronger men than you have been carried away after an hour with me, milord.*

CROMWELL: *Yes, but not feet first!*

MARIE: *Take me in your arms and kiss me again, milord.*

CROMWELL: *Madam please! Someone might come in!*

MARIE: *I don't care! Oh Thomas! Tom! You don't know how unsatisfying my life is! I am like a bottle of good wine that has been left to waste after one sip!*

CROMWELL: *Well, for heaven's sake, put a cork in it!*

(Henry enters)

HENRY: *What goest on here?*

CROMWELL: *Nothing, nothing at all, sire. I was just conversing with her Majesty when she suddenly came over faint and I just corked her in time. I mean, caught her in time.*

HENRY: *Faint? Why should she feel faint?*

CROMWELL: *Lack of fresh air perhaps . . .*

HENRY: *Yes . . . she hasn't been getting any lately.*

CROMWELL: *Oh yes, that too.*

(later—Henry and Bettina dancing)

HENRY: *I expect you got plenty of it [in] Spain, eh?*

BETTINA: *Oh no, they never let me [be] alone with anyone long enough.*

HENRY: *Dancing, I mean.*

BETTINA: *Oh. Oh yes, but it's ver[y] different over there, you know. You se[e] there's these two things . . .*

HENRY: *Yes, I had noticed them.*

BETTINA: *They call them castanets.*

HENRY: *Well, I've heard them calle[d] worse things.*

BETTINA: *And all the time you'r[e] dancing they keep knocking together.*

HENRY: *Yes, I'd noticed that too. It'[s] getting a bit cold in here. Let's go out t[o] the summerhouse and warm up a bit, shal[l] we?*

BETTINA: *Oh no. I know what happen[s] to girls who go into summerhouses with[ ] men.*

HENRY: *Good. That should save a bit o[f] time.*

Abreast of the times, Barbara Windsor has problems in *Carry On Camping*, with Kenneth Williams as the camp leader

Above: Constables Kenneth Williams and Charles Hawtrey in plain dress in *Carry On Constable*

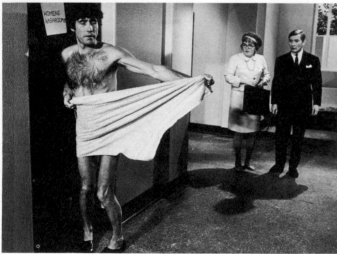

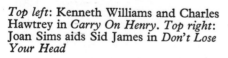

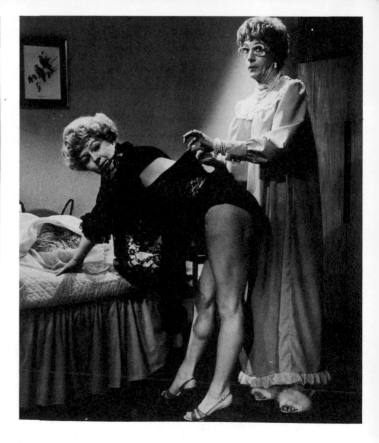

Top left: Kenneth Williams and Charles Hawtrey in *Carry On Henry*. *Top right*: Joan Sims aids Sid James in *Don't Lose Your Head*

Above: Dr Nookey (Jim Dale) interrupted by Patsy Rowlands and Kenneth Williams in *Carry On Again Doctor*

Right: Charles Hawtrey alias Dr Stoppage alias Lady Puddleton assisting Joan Sims 'the moneyed amorous patient'

Sean Connery as James Bond 007 in *Dr. No*

determined to make Bond into a film hero and he and Saltzman went into partnership, forming Eon Productions Ltd. Together they went to United Artists, and after considerable negotiation came away with a 50-50 distribution contract. The biggest battle had yet to be won. United Artists had wanted an established name to play Bond but the producers argued that the books were so vivid in themselves that if they cast well, their James Bond would inevitably become a star; moreover, their way would save much money. They started testing, and among those shortlisted was a tall, fair-haired, rugged actor called Roger Moore. He would have to wait his turn, for the eventual choice was Sean Connery, a jowly, bushy-browed Glaswegian, who had played character parts in a number of totally forgettable films, as well as Shakespeare on the stage, and who, in his time, had been a model of beach clothes, a boxing champion and a chorus boy on tour with *South Pacific*. *Dr No* was a relatively low-budget film, costing around $950,000, although the exotic Jamaican locations and the futuristic sets at Pinewood by Ken Adam gave a contrary impression. The first Bond film was directed by Terence Young, and the sexy co-star, Honey Chile, first seen emerging glistening from the sea was Ursula Andress. From the start the Bond style was established with characters such as M, his enigmatic boss, played by Bernard Lee, and Miss Moneypenny, the infatuated secretary (Lois Maxwell), providing an anchorage of calm assurance through the excessive extravagances of villainy Bond would be called upon to counter. A casual, business-like approach towards the elimination of the opposition was the order—Bond dispatching an enemy with a well-aimed harpoon might mutter an aside 'I think he got the point' which reduced the licensed-to-kill element to a non-sadistic, almost perfunctory routine.

The success of the film was overwhelming, and it meant that successive Bond films acquired bigger and more extravagant production values. *From Russia With Love* was followed by *Goldfinger* (a change of director, this one was by Guy Hamilton) which had a Ken Adam reconstruction of Fort Knox, and *Thunderball*, in which much of the action took place underwater. The creator, Ian Fleming, died soon after the Bond cult really got under way, and thanks to Saltzman and Broccoli his progeny took a prime

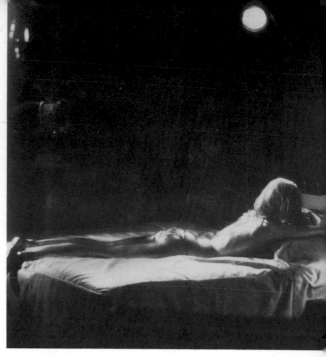

Above: Shirley Eaton painted gold for *Goldfinger*
Left: Helpful attendants in *You Only Live Twice*
Below: Poster for *You Only Live Twice*

Roger Moore takes over the role of 007 in
Live and Let Die and here in
The Man with the Golden Gun

place in the gallery of twentieth-century heroes. Much of the credit was
due to Sean Connery, whose screen presence constantly improved as he
developed nuances of the character, and stayed right outside the conven-
tional heroic mould, by suggesting a seething violence within. There was
also the fascination of the technical gimmickry—the patient exegesis in
many of the films by the armourer as he hands over a normal-looking
attaché case, for instance, which is in reality several deadly weapons, or an
Aston-Martin that can do everything but fly. For *You Only Live Twice*,
directed by Lewis Gilbert, a gigantic volcano was built on the Pinewood
lot, at a cost of £400,000, which absorbed more structural steel than was
used in the building of the high-rise London Hilton. But by now Connery
had had enough, and he backed out of the next Bond film, *On Her Majesty's
Secret Service*, directed by Peter Hunt. The part was taken over by George
Lazenby, an unknown actor attempting a near-impossible task, for the role
had been too definitively coloured by his predecessor. Connery was persuaded to make one more, *Diamonds are Forever*, directed by Guy Hamilton,
who also was to film the next two. Connery finally stepped down, leaving
the field clear for Roger Moore, who to date has made *Live and Let Die* and
The Man with the Golden Gun. At the time of writing preparations are well
under way for *The Spy Who Loved Me*, which may be the most spectacular
Bond film yet. Roger Moore, while physically unlike Connery, has proved
an excellent choice, largely due to the fact that in various television series
he has been able to project a persona wholly in accord with Fleming's
original. In fact, he is much closer to the Bond of the written word than
Connery, and has in no way diminished the potent effect of the films.

7 At The Crossroads

THE Bond pictures represented just a few of the major international movies made at Pinewood in the 'sixties. American companies looked to Britain as a place for making big films more economically than in Hollywood, with the additional bonus of Eady money to be gained if the work qualified as British. So hard ticket pictures such as *Those Magnificent Men in Their Flying Machines*, made by Twentieth Century-Fox in Todd-AO, with Ken Annakin directing a massive star cast in a lavish comedy about an air race between London and Paris in 1910, and for which many flyable replicas of ancient aircraft had to be constructed, Anthony Mann's *The Heroes of Telemark*, with Kirk Douglas and Richard Harris leading an expedition into Nazi-occupied Norway to smash a heavy water factory, Ken Hughes's juvenile fantasy *Chitty Chitty Bang Bang* for United Artists and Cubby Broccoli, and Saltzman and Ben Fisz's epic, *The Battle of Britain*, directed by Guy Hamilton, were among the Studios' major productions. The Fox film *Dr Doolittle*, with Rex Harrison and directed by Richard Fleischer, was started at Pinewood, but was beset by the *Cleopatra* syndrome. After a frustratingly damp summer at Castle Combe, Wiltshire, which had been got up to look like the mythical seaport of Puddleby, the producers cut their losses and shifted the entire production back to Hollywood. The finished film lost heavily, but there was no cause for *schadenfreude* on the part of the British film industry, because in the uncertain climate of American production, in which all the major studios with the exception of Disney had been losing fortunes, anglophobia set in, compounded when *The Battle of Britain* failed to make any impact in America.

Universal had started an interesting but short-lived programme of features under the control of their London production chief, Jay Kanter. Regrettably of the dozen or so films made, not one was a success at the box office, even though star names such as Marlon Brando and Albert Finney were involved. Four of the productions were filmed at Pinewood

Opposite page, above: Stuart Whitman wing walks while Sarah Miles handles the controls in *Those Magnificent Men in their Flying Machines*
Below: Old-time Brooklands reconstructed for the same film

Above: Kirk Douglas and Richard Harris in Anthony Mann's *The Heroes of Telemark*

Fahrenheit 451 directed by François Truffaut. Bee Duffell dies in the book-burning

Chaplin directing Marlon Brando and Sophia Loren in *The Countess from Hong Kong*

Richard Johnson menaced by Daliah Lavi
and Bebe Loncar in *Some Girls Do*

and in the summer of 1966 François Truffaut was shooting his *Fahrenheit 451* on one stage, while on the next Charles Chaplin was directing Brando and Sophia Loren in his ill-fated last film, *The Countess from Hong Kong*. Truffaut was asked if he had been next door to see Charlot. 'No,' he answered, 'what could I say to him?' In the event both films failed but for different reasons. While it was clear that Chaplin's approach was too precise, formalised and inflexible for an actor of Brando's creativity to cope with, resulting in an uncharacteristically wooden, mechanical performance, Truffaut was ill at ease away from his native heath. Ray Bradbury's story of a future where books are forbidden enabled Truffaut to pursue his constant theme of the loner seeking a different society from the one in which he finds himself, and the photography by Nicolas Roeg was imaginative and intriguing—this world did not look so different from our own—but errors of casting, particularly with the leading characters played by Julie Christie and Oskar Werner, helped deaden the impact, although the public had a hard time passing judgement as the film was scarcely given a release. The other two pictures were Peter Hall's first, *Work is a Four Letter Word*, with David Warner, and based on Henry Livings' *Eh?*, and *Charlie Bubbles* which Albert Finney directed and played in, a well-rendered study of estrangement and isolation as a successful writer returns to his roots. Again it was scarcely shown outside the West End.

There were many films following in the wake of James Bond, utilising the spy-secret agent theme, a lot of them shot at Pinewood. Bond producer Harry Saltzman was also responsible for three films based on Len Deighton's spy, the shabby down-at-heel Harry Palmer, who was a kind of other ranks' version of the Fleming hero. Michael Caine played him very satisfactorily in *The Ipcress File*, directed by Sidney J. Furie, *Funeral in Berlin* (Guy Hamilton) and *Billion Dollar Brain* (Ken Russell before notoriety set in). There were also *Hot Enough for June*, with Dirk Bogarde finding himself unwittingly cast as an agent (Ralph Thomas), *Deadlier than the Male* and *Some Girls Do* (again Ralph Thomas) with Richard Johnson playing a latterday Bulldog Drummond, and one sequence of the poor mélange that made up the multi-directed *Casino Royale*, specifically the sec-

Michael Caine in *The Ipcress File*

tion directed by John Huston, with David Niven. Pinewood was to be where the highly successful revived television series, *The Avengers*, was filmed— a product of the Bond cult rejuvenated in 1976 by its creators, Brian Clemens and Albert Fennell. Stanley Donen made *Arabesque*, with Gregory Peck and a sumptuously garbed Sophia Loren, and Jack Smight, *Kaleidoscope* with Warren Beatty and Susannah York. And within the idiom must also be counted Ivan Foxwell and Michael Anderson's *The Quiller Memorandum* with George Segal, Etienne Perrier's *When Eight Bells Toll*, Basil Dearden's jolly period piece *The Assassination Bureau* and John Huston's mood-laden *The Mackintosh Man*.

Telly Savalas and Curt Jurgens in
The Assassination Bureau

Action at Hawkinge—a raid scene from *The Battle of Britain*

Wedding scene from Norman Jewison's film of the award-winning musical *Fiddler on the Roof*

Among recent visiting directors from Hollywood Billy Wilder and Alfred Hitchcock probably tower higher than most. The former made *The Private Life of Sherlock Holmes*, with Robert Stephens as the detective and Colin Blakely as Watson. It was an amusing reappraisal, daring to postulate the thought that Holmes might be homosexual, and larded with Wilderian wit. Another jokey approach to the great crime solver is provided in the new film, *The Seven Per Cent Solution*, directed by Herbert Ross. Hitchcock's return to Pinewood (he had made *Young and Innocent* there in 1937) was with an English murder story, *Frenzy*, with Jon Finch as the suspect and Barry Foster as the strangler. The script was by Anthony Shaffer, who also adapted his long-running play *Sleuth* for Joseph L. Mankiewicz to direct with Laurence Olivier and Michael Caine. His brother Peter's play, *The Royal Hunt of the Sun* was also filmed with Robert Shaw and Christopher Plummer, directed by Irving Lerner.

During the 'sixties Bryan Forbes made three Pinewood films before going to the old Associated British studios at Elstree (which had become part of the EMI organisation) as head of production, perhaps the hottest seat in the British film industry but which he nevertheless held for eighteen months. His Pinewood films were *The Wrong Box*, a Robert Louis Stevenson story with an astonishing cast that included Peter Sellers, Ralph Richardson, Tony Hancock, Michael Caine, Cicely Courtneidge, Nanette Newman, Peter Cook and Dudley Moore, and Wilfrid Lawson in his last role, superb as an inebriated butler; *The Whisperers*, an excellent study of old age with Dame Edith Evans as a pensioner suffering from her own delusions and the heartlessness of others; and *Deadfall*, a crisp thriller again with Michael Caine, and the last film made by Eric Portman before his death. Of the 'old faithfuls' must be numbered the former Ealing director, Basil Dearden, who made *All Night Long*, a modern story about jazz musicians with an Othello plot, *The Mindbenders*, with Dirk Bogarde as the victim of a security process involving total immersion in water to change his personality, *Woman of Straw* with Gina Lollobrigida and Sean Connery, *A Place to Go*, set in Bethnal Green, with Rita Tushingham and Michael Sarne, *Masquerade* with Jack Hawkins involved in a kidnap plot, and his most interesting film, *Khartoum*, with Charlton Heston as General Gordon and Laurence Olivier as the Mahdi, complete with dusky skin, rolling eyes and heavy accent.

Val Guest was another industry stalwart, having begun in the 'thirties as a screenwriter for the Will Hay films. He made *80,000 Suspects* with Richard Johnson and Claire Bloom coping with an outbreak of plague in the unlikely setting of Bath, *The Beauty Jungle*, an exposé of the beauty

Opposite page: Gregory Peck and Sophia
Loren in *Arabesque*
Right: Alfred Hitchcock, directing his
second Pinewood film *Frenzy*
Below: A three-dimensional Jon Finch in
Frenzy

Above: John Mills in *The Wrong Box*, from the story by Robert Louis Stevenson

Below: Charlton Heston as General Gordon dies in *Khartoum*

Opposite page: Laurence Olivier as a
swarthy Mahdi in *Khartoum*

Edith Evans in Bryan Forbes'
The Whisperers

queen business with Ian Hendry and Janette Scott, and *Toomorrow*, a combination of pop musical and science fiction which brought the delectable Australian, Olivia Newton-John, to the screen. Ronald Neame made *The Prime of Miss Jean Brodie*, a Muriel Spark story with Maggie Smith as an Edinburgh schoolteacher. Hayley Mills got her first screen kiss from Peter McEnery in Walt Disney's *The Moonspinners*, a thriller set on Crete and directed by James Neilsen, noteworthy for bringing the siren of the silent screen, Pola Negri, out of retirement and to Pinewood. Hayley was later directed by her father, John Mills, in a rather unpleasant rustic story, *Sky West and Crooked*, while Peter McEnery fought valiantly for Susan Hampshire in another Disney film, a costumed rip-roarer, Michael O'Herlihy's *The Fighting Prince of Donegal*. Cornel Wilde had earlier filmed an Arthurian romance, *Lancelot and Guinevere*, the sets later being used with splendid economy for Dick Lester's *The Mouse on the Moon*.

Peter Brook transferred his Royal Shakespeare production of the Peter Weiss play *The Persecution and Assassination of Jean-Paul Marat as Performed by the Inmates of the Asylum of Charenton under the Direction of the Marquis de Sade* to the screen and quite apart from having the longest title on record, it turned out to be more than a mere carbon copy of the stage original, although essentially a work of considerable theatricality. Similarly, Paul Czinner filmed the Royal Ballet production of *Romeo and Juliet* with Margot Fonteyn, Rudolph Nureyev and David Blair dancing to Kenneth Macmillan's choreography and Prokofiev's music.

An exception to the steady stream of failures in America of Pinewood films was Columbia's *To Sir With Love*, directed by James Clavell and starring Sidney Poitier as a black immigrant schoolteacher winning approval from his underprivileged East End pupils. It proved to be one of the biggest grossing pictures of its year, and it was hard to see why, as so many other subjects with a British background had died in the United States. Ken Russell's *The Devils*, an explosion of orgiastic suffering, berserk nuns, torture and excess at the court of Louis XIII was another box-office winner, its impact heightened by the artificial secrecy shrouding the actual filming.

Towards the end of the 'sixties it was clear that the Americans were overinvesting in British production. Their £15 million in 1965 had leaped to over £20 million in 1967, and worried voices were expressing concern at the possibility of a withdrawal, which would particularly affect the NFFC, now having almost reached breakeven point. Then at the end of the decade M-G-M suddenly sold their large Borehamwood Studios, moving production to the older and less efficient Elstree Studios down the road, where EMI were now in control. Three years later M-G-M closed down its

Olivia Newton-John gets up in Val Guest's
Toomorrow

British operation entirely, passing distribution to Cinema International Corporation, which also distributed Paramount and Universal films, and giving Elstree a very perilous future. It was a remarkable achievement that in the same year The Rank Organisation was able to announce record profits of £15 million, an increase of 31 per cent on the year before. It was not the first time that the copying machines had come to the rescue.

Pinewood had to make many adjustments to stay in line with the convulsions of the British film industry. The managing director of the studios, E.A.R. (Kip) Herren, who had succeeded Spencer Reis, becoming general manager in 1959 and managing director in 1966, said at the time of the 30th anniversary: 'We have made, and indeed are continuing to make, some of the world's finest motion pictures at Pinewood Studios. And that says all that is necessary about the past and the present. Our thinking in the future must be universal.' Certainly there had been many improvements to make Pinewood Studios more flexible. In 1964 stage H had been built specially for MCA TV production in the short time between May and September, by when it was possible to move a unit of 150 people into a self-contained administration block with dressing rooms, hairdressing, makeup and wardrobe departments. The first series to be shot there was *Court Martial*, consisting of 26 48-minute films, each produced in $9\frac{1}{2}$ days.

Maggie Smith takes exception to Robert
Stephens in *The Prime of Miss Jean Brodie*

Then followed J and K Stages, both large ones, 110ft by 80ft, and L and M, which were 105ft by 90ft. These were remarkable buildings, designed on a dual purpose principle, so that they could be used for television as well as films. It meant special floors, for the traditional wood flooring in most film studios into which nails are constantly hammered would interfere with the smooth flow of the TV dollies. Just as when Pinewood was built in the 'thirties, careful studies were made of other studios throughout the world in order to incorporate the most up-to-date ideas, and to anticipate future trends. The overhead grid was built to take monopole lighting systems with lightweight lamps, all capable of remote control adjustment, while sound equipment, mixing consoles and closed-circuit television all reflected the wish to be in the vanguard of studio design. But most remarkable of all has been the fact that Pinewood has actually expanded in recent years, at a time when film studios all over the world have closed or reduced in size. In Britain, of the big four in the 'sixties—Borehamwood, Shepperton, Elstree and Pinewood—Borehamwood was sold off for development, Shepperton was reduced in size from 60 acres to 20, with only four of the original 13 stages left for film-making, and Elstree similarly shrank. Both of these studios changed to the 'four walls' system, whereby a production company rents the space and then contracts separately for additional facilities, thus drastically reducing the permanent staff required, as well as offering a more economic method of studio leasing than the traditional method of a fully-serviced studio, with all its overheads. Pinewood is, consequently, the only British studio left that functions on this basis. It is generally regarded that there can in the future be room for only one such studio, and its presence is essential if the British film industry is to continue to exist. Many films are made entirely on location, but the studio is still needed for editing, dubbing and other post-production areas.

Even though there was a drastic reduction of the inflow of American money in the 'seventies, it was still more economical for Paramount to move their production of *The Great Gatsby* to Pinewood, rather than California, after location shooting at Newport, Rhode Island. Jack Clayton's film was released in the United States with the usual credit line 'Made at Pinewood Studios, London, England' omitted, so that audiences would not think it was a British film. Another American film of considerable proportions which was made with Pinewood as its base, with locations in Munich, was Norman Jewison's *Rollerball*. Jewison had previously directed the big musical, *Fiddler on the Roof*, another Pinewood major production.

Television has also been a major element in the recent Pinewood story. One of the most elaborate drama productions was Screen Gems' six-hour

Sidney Poitier with Christian Robins in
To Sir With Love, directed by James Clavell

version of the Leon Uris book, *QBVII*. Series made at Pinewood have
included *The Persuaders*, *The Zoo Gang*, *The Strange Report* and *Space
1999*, while one-off specials have been made of George Cukor's *Love
Among the Ruins*, Anthony Harvey's *The Glass Menagerie* and a remake of
Brief Encounter with Richard Burton and Sophia Loren.

The logistics of Pinewood are formidable. The scene dock, for instance,
is the largest in the world. It has 2000 assorted doors, 15,000 windows.
There is a vacuum-forming press that can mass-produce almost anything
in plastic, while the carpenters' shop has performed miracles of construction—probably their finest hour being when Harry Saltzman and Ben
Fisz were making *The Battle of Britain* and a production line of fake

Hurricanes had to be set up worthy of the efforts of Lord Beaverbrook in 1940. The exterior tank is the largest in Europe, and is about an acre in extent, with a capacity of 800,000 gallons. Behind it is a backdrop 260 feet long and 60 feet high. The tank is often used by visiting film companies who may not be making the rest of the film at Pinewood, such as Dick Lester's *Juggernaut*, which was a Twickenham film. The sound department is proud of the Oscar for Best Sound awarded to Norman Jewison's *Fiddler on the Roof*, which was recorded in Theatre 2. The equipment in the dubbing theatres is up to date, costly and complex, while Theatre 7 is not only the most luxurious of the viewing theatres, with 83 individual Pullman seats arranged on a tiered floor, but has adjoining it a complex which includes a dozen cutting rooms, the most modern of the 46 at Pinewood. Electricity to run the Studios comes from a power house equipped with seven diesel generators. Something like 400,000 units are consumed each year, more than enough to light a small town, but energy-saving schemes convert a lot of waste heat.

Even catering is a highly organised section of the studios. Quite apart from regular lunches, up to 250 a day in the restaurant and 1000 in the two cafeterias, the department is on 24-hour call, and can with the aid of six mobile kitchens feed thousands of extras on location. Quite often the BBC has contracted Pinewood location catering services for their own major productions. The department is also responsible for providing and preparing food used in films themselves, and Tommy Thomas, the catering manager, has had to supply, for instance, 4000 cream buns for a slapstick fight in a Norman Wisdom film and an evil-smelling seal carcass for Nicholas Ray's *Savage Innocents*, in which Anthony Quinn played an Eskimo.

Another of Pinewood's Oscars went to Charles Staffell, head of the special process department. Not awarded for any film in particular, but as a general tribute to the inventiveness and sophistication of the department, it was the first general technical award made by the Academy to Britain. Constant changes in front and back projection technique have been applied to keep Pinewood ahead in the game. One of their showpieces is a triple-head projector which, when not in use at Pinewood, has been packed up and carted off to other studios, and even abroad. With it, composite scenes can be shot, often so brilliantly that even expert eyes have failed to distinguish which parts have been added by projection. Over the years there has been a steady reduction in focal lengths of lenses, as well as improvements in the material from which the screens are made.

Jack Clayton directs Robert Redford and
Mia Farrow in *The Great Gatsby*

Above: James Caan with John Houseman.
A scene from Norman Jewison's *Rollerball*
Below: James Caan plays *Rollerball*

But for all Pinewood's excellence, its future remains uncertain. Among recent major films made there must be mentioned *Gold*, *The Wilby Conspiracy*, *That Lucky Touch*, Disney's *One of Our Dinosaurs is Missing* and *Escape from the Dark*, *Mister Quilp*, *Sarah* with Glenda Jackson, *Bugsy Malone*, John Dark's production of *At the Earth's Core* and Bryan Forbes's highly acclaimed musical of Cinderella, *The Slipper and the Rose*. Nevertheless, in the last financial year, Pinewood was £450,000 in the red. Part of the decreased earnings were due to the effect of changed taxation laws on foreign nationals resident in Britain and on overseas earnings of British nationals, which seriously affected the film industry, and made Britain a

Leonard Frey, Norma Cranc and Topol in
Fiddler on the Roof

A rapturous audience greeting Glenda
Jackson as Sarah Bernhardt in *Sarah*

Above: Director Bryan Forbes with the
cast of *The Slipper and the Rose*
Below: Richard Chamberlain and Gemma
Craven in *The Slipper and the Rose*—the
story of Cinderella

Above: Scott Baio and Florrie Dogger, two of the young faces in *Bugsy Malone*
Below: Chorus line in *Bugsy Malone*—a speakeasy of the Twenties

less attractive country in which to work. Inflation and the depressed state of the economy were other factors. Yet during the three-day-week period of 1974 Pinewood kept working normally. In 1975, the then Prime Minister Harold Wilson, recalling his earlier involvement with the setting up of the NFFC in the post-war period, established a working party under the NFFC's managing director, John Terry. Its proposals, although hardly radical, did allow for the injection of a further £5 million into the corporation, public money which could, if sensibly applied, make a difference to the industry as a whole. Films have always represented an uncertain area of public involvement, bridging an awkward gap between art and commerce. Artistic merit has often been at odds with public taste of the time, and gone unrecognised at the box office. Hence the constant search for the compromise between the two, and the retreat into surefire propositions, be they spin-offs from well-known television series or exploitation pictures designed for the X certificate market. To his credit, the chairman of The Rank Organisation, Sir John Davis, for years resisted the latter category of films, but inevitably they eventually became fodder at the Odeons. A policy of tripling and twinning existing theatres, instead of closing them, had meant that more screens were available for specialised films in smaller auditoriums. Unfortunately, too often it meant the cheap, exploitation pictures, rather than art.

Lord Rank, founder of the studios and the organisation that bears his name, died after retirement in 1972.

Now Pinewood ends its first 40 years with various question marks. How long can it survive in its present form? Will it, like Elstree and Shepperton, have to follow a four walls policy? Has the constant decline in admissions to cinemas now bottomed out? Can the British film industry produce the kind of world money-spinning films such as *Jaws*, *The Exorcist*, *The Godfather Part II* and *The French Connection*, which have done so much to bolster the declined fortunes of Hollywood in recent years?

What *is* for sure is that if such a film can be made, then Pinewood is the logical place in which to do it, because it is where most of the technical and craft skills left in the British film industry are now concentrated. As Kip Herren, its managing director, unequivocally says: 'Pinewood *is* the British film industry.'

Acknowledgements

Many people have co-operated in enabling this book to be written, designed and produced at rapid speed so that it could be published in time for Pinewood's 40th anniversary. Particular thanks are due to Kip Herren, Cyril Howard and Norman Martlew at Pinewood Studios who gave me their time freely and smoothed many corners. My thanks also to the British Film Institute, John Kobal, the Cinema Bookshop, Barbara de Lord of Fox-Rank Distributors Ltd, Graham Smith of Cinema International and United Artists for supplying those stills that did not come from the massive collection at Pinewood itself, and to Sid Colin for supplying *Carry On* material. Every effort has been made to trace the copyright holders of the photographs and quoted material. Should there be any omissions in this respect, we apologise and shall be pleased to make the appropriate acknowledgement in future editions.

I am especially grateful to Jenny Towndrow for her inspiration and encouragement, Colin Webb and Kate Dunning of Elm Tree Books for their professionalism and unflagging enthusiasm through all stages of production, Tewfick Codsi for the long hours he spent on the design and layout, Penny King for typing the manuscript, Rosie Franklin, my secretary, for the efficient tying together of the loose ends, and my wife Fran, for her constant patience and the sharing of much midnight oil.

Finally, this book is dedicated to all those remarkable men and women who in 40 years have worked at Pinewood, be they stars or tea ladies, producers or clapperboys. They all helped to make movies from the mansion.

George Perry
London   July 1976

Bibliography

Balcon, Michael, *Michael Balcon Presents . . .: A Lifetime of Films*, Hutchinson, 1969

Betts, Ernest, *The Film Business*, George Allen and Unwin, 1973

Board of Trade, *Report of a Committee of Enquiry on the Distribution and Exhibition of Cinema Films*, HMSO, 1949

Board of Trade, *Report of the Film Studio Committee*, HMSO, 1948

Board of Trade, *Report of the Working Party on Film Production Costs*, HMSO, 1949

Board of Trade, *Tendencies to Monopoly in the Cinematograph Film Industry*, HMSO, 1944

Butler, Ivan, *Cinema in Britain: an Illustrated Survey*, Tantivy, 1973

Durgnat, Raymond, *A Mirror for England*, Faber, 1970

Forbes, Bryan, *Notes for a Life*, Collins, 1974

Gibbon, Mark, *The Red Shoes Ballet: A Critical Study*, Saturn Press, 1968

Gifford, Denis, *British Cinema*, Zwemmer, 1968

Gifford, Denis, *The British Film Catalogue 1895–1970*, David and Charles, 1973

Hinxman, Margaret and D'Arcy, Susan, *The Films of Dirk Bogarde*, Literary Services, 1974

Huntley, John, *British Technicolor Films*, Skelton Robinson, 1948

Kelly, Terence; Norton, Graham and Perry, George, *A Competitive Cinema*, Institute of Economic Affairs, 1966

Manvell, Roger, *New Cinema in Britain*, Studio Vista, 1969

Manvell, Roger, *Twenty Years of British Films, 1925–1945*, Falcon Press, 1947

Mosley, Leonard, *The Battle of Britain, the Making of the Film*, Weidenfeld and Nicolson, 1969

Oakley, Charles, *Where We Came In*, George Allen and Unwin, 1964

PEP, *The British Film Industry*, Political and Economical Planning, 1952

Perry, George, *The Great British Picture Show*, Hart-Davis, MacGibbon, 1974

Pratley, Gerald, *The Cinema of David Lean*, Tantivy, 1974

Sharp, Dennis, *The Picture Palace*, Hugh Evelyn, 1969

Shipman, David, *The Great Movie Stars—The Golden Years*, Hamlyn, 1970

Shipman, David, *The Great Movie Stars—The International Years*, Angus and Robertson, 1972

Spraos, John, *The Decline of the Cinema*, George Allen and Unwin, 1962

Walker, Alexander, *Hollywood, England*, Michael Joseph, 1974

Wilcox, Herbert, *Twenty-five Thousand Sunsets*, The Bodley Head, 1967

Wood, Alan, *Mr. Rank*, Hodder and Stoughton, 1952

Pinewood Films

1936

London Melody (part)
Talk of the Devil
Splinters in the Air Force
The Scarab Murder Mystery
Our Fighting Navy
Melody and Romance
Cross My Heart
The Gang Show

1937

Midnight Menace
Holiday's End
The Frog
Cavalier of the Streets
Sunset in Vienna
Museum Piece
The Fatal Hour
Jericho
Gangway
Night Ride
Smash and Grab
Young and Innocent
The Sky's the Limit
The Last Curtain
Command Performance
Sweet Devil
Missing from Home
Break the News
Sailing Along
Lancashire Luck
Follow Your Star
Kicking the Moon Around
Strange Boarders
Incident in Shanghai

1938

Crackerjack
Pygmalion
A Spot of Bother
This Man is News
Keep Smiling
A Stolen Life
Lightning Conductor
The Mikado
St Paul
Climbing High
So This is London
Lambeth Walk
Inspector Hornleigh
The Greatest of These
Beyond Our Horizon

1946

Great Expectations (part)
Green for Danger
Black Narcissus
Take My Life
Captain Boycott

1947

The End of the River
The Woman in the Hall
Blanche Fury
The Red Shoes
Oliver Twist
Esther Waters

1948

London Belongs to Me
The Passionate Friends
The Blue Lagoon
Once a Jolly Swagman
All Over the Town
Once Upon a Dream
Fools Rush In
Warning to Wantons
Floodtide
Obsession

1949

The Golden Salamander
Madeleine
The Spider and the Fly
Boys in Brown
The Astonished Heart
So Long at the Fair
Dear Mr Prohack
Prelude to Fame
Stop Press Girl
Poet's Pub

1950

Waterfront Conqueror
Tony Draws a Horse
Trio
The Clouded Yellow
The Woman in Question
The Adventurers
Highly Dangerous
Blackmailed
The Browning Version
Night Without Stars

1951

White Corridors
Hotel Sahara
High Treason
Valley of the Eagles
Appointment with Venus
Encore
Hunted
The Card
The Importance of Being Earnest
Penny Princess

1952

Something Money Can't Buy
Meet Me Tonight
The Planter's Wife
Venetian Bird
It Started in Paradise
Made in Heaven
The Long Memory
The Sword and the Rose
The Net
Top of the Form
Desperate Moment
Genevieve
The Malta Story
The Final Test
Turn the Key Softly

1953

Always a Bride
Personal Affair
Hell Below Zero
A Day to Remember
The Million Pound Note
You Know What Sailors Are
The Kidnappers
Trouble in Store
Fast and Loose
The Black Knight
Doctor in the House
Forbidden Cargo
The Beachcomber
The Seekers

1954

The Purple Plain
Up to His Neck
The Young Lovers
Mad About Men
Simba
One Good Turn
To Paris With Love
As Long as They're Happy
Passage Home
Above Us the Waves
The Prisoner

1955

Value for Money
Doctor at Sea
A Woman for Joe
Man of the Moment
An Alligator Named Daisy
Simon and Laura
All for Mary
A Town Like Alice
Lost
Reach for the Sky
The Black Tent
Jumping for Joy
The Battle of the River Plate

1956

Jacqueline
Eyewitness
The Spanish Gardener
House of Secrets
Checkpoint
Tiger in the Smoke
The Secret Place
True as a Turtle
The Prince and the Showgirl
The Iron Petticoat
Up in the World
Ill Met by Moonlight
High Tide at Noon
Doctor at Large

1957

Hell Drivers
Miracle in Soho
Across the Bridge
Robbery Under Arms
Campbell's Kingdom
Dangerous Exile
The One That Got Away
Seven Thunders
Windom's Way
The Gypsy and the Gentleman
Just My Luck
A Tales of Two Cities
Violent Playground
Carve Her Name With Pride
Innocent Sinners
Rooney
A Night to Remember
The Wind Cannot Read
The Naked Truth
The Heart of a Child
The Abominable Snowman

1958

Nor the Moon by Night
Sea Fury
Rockets Galore
The Passionate Summer
Floods of Fear
Sea of Sand
Bachelor of Hearts
The Square Peg
The Captain's Table
Operation Amsterdam
Too Many Crooks
Whirlpool
The Thirty-Nine Steps
Tiger Bay
Ferry to Hong Kong
Sapphire
Carry On Sergeant
The Sheriff of Fractured Jaw
Carry On Nurse

1959

The Heart of a Man
The Royal Ballet
Upstairs and Downstairs
Carry On Teacher
Peeping Tom
Carry On Constable
The League of Gentlemen
North West Frontier
Kidnapped
S.O.S. Pacific
Sink the Bismarck!
Please Turn Over
Follow a Star
Conspiracy of Hearts
Der Rosenkavalier
Gulliver's Travels
Dentist in the Chair

1960

Make Mine Mink
Sons and Lovers
Never Let Go
Doctor in Love
The Singer not the Song
The Professionals
He Stole a Million
Man in the Moon
Piccadilly Third Stop
There Was a Crooked Man
Watch Your Stern
Hellfire Club
No Love for Johnnie
The Bulldog Breed
No Kidding
The Impersonator
The Treasure of Monte Cristo
Cleopatra (abandoned)

1961

Carry On Regardless
Flame in the Streets
Whistle Down the Wind
Victim
No My Darling Daughter
Raising the Wind
The Long Shadow
What a Whopper
In the Doghouse
All Night Long
The Waltz of the Toreadors
Tiara Tahiti
A Pair of Briefs

1962

The Castaways
Twice Round the Daffodils
A Life for Ruth
Dr No
Carry On Cruising
Play it Cool
The Horse Without a Head
Masters of Venus
The Traitors
The Primitives
Band of Thieves
The Wild and the Willing
Lancelot and Guinevere
The Stranglehold
The Iron Maiden
The Three Lives of Thomasina
The Mindbenders
On the Beat
Mouse on the Moon
Call Me Bwana
Nurse on Wheels

1963

The Informers
The Bay of St Michel
80,000 Suspects
A Place to Go
Farewell Performance
The Switch
Bomb in the High Street
Carry On Cabby
Doctor in Distress
Dr Syn
From Russia With Love
Live it Up
A Stitch in Time
Seance on a Wet Afternoon
This is my Street
Woman of Straw
The Moonspinners
Carry on Jack
Blind Corner
Hot Enough for June
The Beauty Jungle

1964

Carry On Spying
Guns at Batasi
Goldfinger
Devils of Darkness
Masquerade
The High Bright Sun
High Wind in Jamaica
Carry On Cleo
The Secret of Blood Island
The Legend of Young Dick
   Turpin
The Ipcress File
Three Hats for Lisa
City in the Sea
The Early Bird

1965

Those Magnificent Men in their
   Flying Machines
The Intelligence Men
The Heroes of Telemark
The Big Job
Thunderball
Sky West and Crooked
Arabesque
Carry On Cowboy
Khartoum
The Fighting Prince of Donegal
The Wrong Box
Romeo and Juliet
Doctor in Clover
Deadline for Diamonds
Stop the World—I Want to Get
   Off
Manutara

1966

That Riviera Touch
The Silicates
Carry On Screaming
Kaleidoscope
Fahrenheit 451
The Countess from Hong Kong
Casino Royale (part)
The Quiller Memorandum
The Whisperers
Funeral in Berlin
Deadlier than the Male
Marat/Sade
Finders Keepers
You Only Live Twice
To Sir With Love
Dr Doolittle (abandoned)
Don't Lose Your Head
The Magnificent Two
The Long Duel

1967

Charlie Bubbles
Billion Dollar Brain
Work is a Four-Letter Word
Pretty Polly
Night of the Big Heat
A Challenge for Robin Hood
Follow that Camel
Deadfall
Prudence and the Pill
Chitty Chitty Bang Bang
Carry On Doctor
The Limbo Line
Nobody Runs Forever

1968

The Assassination Bureau
Carry On . . . Up the Khyber
Dracula has Risen from the Grave
The Battle of Britain
The Prime of Miss Jean Brodie
Some Girls Do
Doppelganger
The Most Dangerous Man in the
   World
The Anniversary
Carry On Camping
On Her Majesty's Secret Service

1969

Connecting Rooms
The Private Life of Sherlock
   Holmes
David Copperfield
Toomorrow
Tam Lin
Perfect Friday
When Eight Bells Toll
Carry On Up the Jungle

1970

Doctor in Trouble
Cause for Alarm
Carry On Loving
The Devil's Touch
Jane Eyre
Assault
Zeppelin
Fiddler on the Roof
Countess Dracula
The Devils
Quest
Carry On Henry
Revenge

1971

200 Motels
Hands of the Ripper
Nobody Ordered Love
Carry On At Your Convenience
The Magnificent 7 Deadly Sins
All Coppers Are
Please Sir
Diamonds are Forever
Frenzy
Madame Sin
Vampire Circus
Baffled
Lady Caroline Lamb
Carry On Matron
Doomwatch

1972

Innocent Bystanders
Nothing But the Night
A Warm December
Carry On Abroad
Sleuth
The Amazing Mr Blunden
That's Your Funeral
Nightmare Rally
Bless This House
Nearest and Dearest

Never Mind the Quality, Feel the Width
Phase IV
The Day of the Jackal
The Belstone Fox
The Mackintosh Man
Live and Let Die

1973

No Sex Please We're British
Carry On Girls
The Great Gatsby
The Abdication
11 Harrowhouse

1974

Gold
The Ghoul
Carry On Dick
The Wilby Conspiracy

Mr Quilp
The Man with the Golden Gun
Rollerball
One of our Dinosaurs is Missing
That Lucky Touch

1975

Carry On Behind
The Bawdy Adventures of Tom Jones
The Slipper and the Rose
Bugsy Malone
Sarah
The Seven Per Cent Solution
Escape from the Dark

1976

At the Earth's Core
Carry On England
Candleshoe
The Spy Who Loved Me

Index